A Mother's
Wounded Heart

Tina Edens

Aster Press
Blue Fortune Enterprises LLC

A MOTHER'S WOUNDED HEART
Copyright © 2021 by Tina Edens.

All rights reserved. Printed in the United States of America. No part of this book may be used or reproduced in any manner whatsoever without written permission except in the case of brief quotations embodied in critical articles or reviews.

Thank you for buying an authorized edition of this book and for complying with copyright laws by not reproducing, scanning or distributing any portion of the contents without written permission.

This story, experiences and words are the author's.

For information contact :
Blue Fortune Enterprises, LLC
Aster Press
P.O. Box 554
Yorktown, VA 23690
http://blue-fortune.com

Book and Cover design by BFE, LLC

ISBN: 978-1-948979-73-3
First Edition: November 2021

*Dedicated to all Mothers in the world
with a Wounded Heart*

Prologue

It is common to think that women are looked at as somewhat of a superhero in the family. As women, we carry the future of this world. We are the protectors of the generations to come. As mothers, we don't often show the internal battle happening in our hearts while trying to maintain a normal life with our husband and children, every day doubting the decisions that we make about situations that pop up in life. We heap mental abuse on ourselves, wondering if we are raising our children correctly or if we are living in our truth.

Many kids in the world today, as in generations past, have experienced things in their family dynamics such as sexual abuse, emotional abuse, drug abuse, physical abuse, abandonment, and the death of a loved one at young ages. Children have had to make adult decisions at very early ages because children are raising children. Even kid's television shows display adult behaviors that influence their daily decisions. Many children are confused by what they see in society, while feeling as though it is their fault for the drama in their lives, which naturally affects family dynamics.

I have noticed many children listen to TV shows more than they listen to their parents, sometimes causing the child to argue that the content is truth and not fiction. This happens because parents allow children to spend free time watching television instead of going outside so they can use their imagination. Since children don't necessarily understand the content they are watching, they tend to mirror the behavior of that show. When disciplined by parents for mimicking this behavior, this causes inner conflict for the child, creating feelings of brokenness and assuming they are at fault for the drama occurring in their family dynamics.

Take a moment and look at the decisions you have made in your life. Some decisions you are proud of and some you regret you ever made. We teach our children what we know, which is based on the lessons that we learned in life from what our parents taught us and what they learned from their experiences. I call this a generational chain of events. When an individual is able to break that chain of events in their generation, they in turn stop it for generations to come. This is happening to little boys and girls all around the world. If we as parents are able to show positive ways to overcome situations in our lives, then we are able to break the chains and guide our future for the better.

When we share our experience with other people, we can educate current and future generations based on the results of the decisions we have made and our experiences with those decisions. I consider these lessons "wounds of our heart." There are generations of people not showing the wounds of their hearts, which is passed down to our children. It is so hard to be vulnerable and share the pain that we have suffered. I am here to tell you to share the experience that has brought you to where you are today. If something in your life doesn't make your heart, or you, happy, then let it go. Don't continue to do the things that make you unhappy in life. So when I say let go of what is not making you happy, it doesn't mean that you should let go of everything. Let go of the things that are not serving you for the good. For example, if you are surrounding yourself with people who are always getting into trouble with the law or putting yourself in situations that in your heart and gut you know is completely wrong, let them go. They are not helping you to grow into your true self.

As a child, I was often a follower, because I had been pushed aside by other people in this world. I had been abandoned, unloved, and felt unworthy of being loved since I started my journey on this earth. I longed to not be alone and to have someone I could talk to without judgement. I needed love, not the romantic love, but unconditional love. The love that people should have for all humanity, regardless of gender or race. After all, every person in this world bleeds red.

This book details my spiritual journey through my life and the spiritual growth that I discovered through the tragedy and the beauty of situations that occurred. This story is about several generations of chains being broken. This is my life story of lessons and experiences that I feel need to be shared with all the mothers who have wounded hearts.

There is no manual that guides us to our life's purpose or roadmap that details every turn we should make. This book provides hope to the single mom with three children, hope to the mother who has been divorced, and hope for the mother who has lost a child or children while trying to continue in life with a smile on her face. I have struggled with this lesson on a daily basis. There are people who must know why and need to have not only a Plan A, but a Plan B and a Plan C. That is my personality all the way. I was never given a road map from my biological parents. It is our parents' job to guide us through life decisions while still protecting us from the evil in this world.

This book is about my experiences as a child, an adolescent and then adult. The trials and tribulations that I endured in life because of the choices my mother made still affect me to this day. The pain that was in her heart when I was conceived carried into my heart and has affected my entire life.

Mothers are the reflection of grace, love, and peace in this world. They often forget to give back to themselves so that they can keep balance in their lives. Mothers give so much to the family and work environment. We should always honor our mothers, while understanding that their hearts have been wounded by many things in life and the continual sacrifices they make to support their family's emotional and physical well-being.

While I am on this spiritual journey, I have learned many lessons. Some lessons were of betrayal, pain, love, dishonesty, and grief. The most important lessons have helped me to raise my children into the beautiful souls that they are today by loving them unconditionally. Our life lessons are to be shared with our future generations. As mothers, these lessons of betrayal, pain, love, dishonesty, and grief are the wounds of our hearts that need to be healed.

Mothers have experiences that leave scars within their heart. The good thing is that a scar will heal, but with every scar, there is a lesson that can be learned and passed down from generation to generation. There are women who endure more pain than others. It is my belief that those women are the ones who break the chain of their ancestral history of suffering and teach the younger generations to break the chains of their mother's wounded heart.

My life has been unpredictable, like the wind. There are times when the wind is calm. On the good days, there is a little breeze, a perfect breeze combined with a moderate temperature. Other days, when my life is not going right, the wind blows like a raging storm. The best way to look at it is as if there is a perfect breeze, then all is well in life. The change in the wind symbolizes the change that needs to happen in life in order for us to grow spiritually.

There is one thing I want to impress upon all women: *never lose hope and faith that the life you want for yourself and your family is within your reach.* You may not see that someone or something is looking after you; however, there is always going to be a light at the end of the tunnel. The best advice I can share with everyone is to love the good *and* the bad in life, because both act as a transformation into the new you.

Thank you for coming on this journey with me.

Tina

Chapter 1
The Beginning of Life

This is a little background of my beginning: my biological mother was 15 years old when she brought me into this world. She was a very smart woman who loved to laugh a lot. She was abused as a child and suffered from depression her entire life. I had heard through the family grapevine that my mother was sexually active at a very young age. She always had a new boyfriend. There was always someone new that she had a crush on or wanted to date.

I personally believe that this behavior was the result of being abused. The depression she suffered from and the lack of self-esteem was probably the hardest thing she dealt with every day of her life, resulting in a feeling of nastiness, that she had been used as a pawn in a man's sexual fantasy, but still thinking it was nice to get attention.

Depression is a very serious disease that can be genetic. It is also a very lonely disease. There needs to be more help for children and adults who deal with depression. Doctors are quick to throw prescription drugs at the problem instead of talking to an individual and figuring out what can be done to help them. I have been in counseling and would always feel like I left the session the same way that I entered. I have found out that if I am able to shut down my brain and listen to what my heart says, I am able to heal my wounds while finding solutions to my problems. While I understand that depression has a range of causes and outcomes, this is simply my personal experience that I am sharing.

As a young adult, my mother made some decisions that a 15-year-old should not have to make. I think she just wanted to be free. To be free of the pain that came with the lack of self-confidence. I feel in my heart as though she was trying to get away from the depression that she fought and she ran to anyone who was willing to show her attention, whether it was good or bad. Her decisions led to her being a pregnant teen. In the 80s, there were a lot of teen pregnancies and girls were often looked down upon in society, as they still are today. My mother's wounds of her heart consisted of embarrassment, shame, guilt, and lack of self-worth. She felt that she would never amount to anything and was bound to have continued devastation in her life.

These feelings led to her giving me up twice before the age of seven. It also didn't help that she never received the type of support she desperately needed during this experience of bringing a child into this world while still being a child herself. This type of behavior was one of my family's generational chains that I have broken. Most of the women in my family had their children very young. In fact, both when my mother was born and later when I was born, there were five living generations of women in my family. So I would think that they would have given her more support during this experience; however, unfortunately, this is one of those chains that was not broken from the past generations for my mother.

People do not understand how hard it is for a mother to carry a baby for the full term and then make the decision to give their child up for adoption. Each mother also had another option: abortion. I personally don't agree with abortion, just because it is a life, a soul, and a human who is in this realm for a reason. When mothers abort a child, they are altering future generations. For example, what if that baby's soul was to grow up and create the cure for cancer or if that baby was supposed to be the President of the United States and put an end to world hunger? Some women are just way too young, and they want a good home for their child. Others are not able to provide the care that the child will need in their lifetime. It doesn't matter the reason a mother would give birth to a child and give it up; the fact is, when a mother makes this decision, it is painful for the mother but a gift of life for the child.

As a child, I could not understand why my mother would give me up. I struggled as a child, like so many who are adopted, feeling worthless, abandoned, and unloved. The thought, "Who is going to love me since my own mother doesn't want me?" was heavy on my heart for many years. I knew then that if I had children, I would never part from them because I didn't want them to feel the way I had while growing to adulthood.

A mother-daughter relationship is like no other and cannot be compared to a father-daughter relationship. A mother is your first and best friend for life. The unconditional love that a mother showers on her children stays with them for the rest of their life. This mother-daughter relationship is the foundation for all other friendships we create in life. The child will never find anyone who loves them as much as their mother. When a child doesn't have this relationship foundation, it will reflect in the decisions that they make in life. The lack of unconditional love that sometimes happens in families with foster children, orphans, and adopted children is what I believe steers them onto the wrong path.

My story begins from the first moments I remember, which was in 1987: I was three years old. It was summer in Florida, the beautiful sunshine state. My biological mother had decided to place me with a family that she thought might be my father's so that she could drive a truck with a man she had met. My mother was again running from her responsibilities in search of her soul's purpose. Anytime something bad happened in her life, she would run away in order to have peace in her mind and not acknowledge the consequences of her decisions. I believe that she felt she was doing the right thing by giving me to one of her lovers, who she thought was my father. She left my life for about three years.

This is what I can now remember, which I have found out that I had mentally blocked because it was such a painful experience. It is amazing how our mind can block situations from our memory, a coping skill because it is so painful to the heart. Women are able to tap into this ability, because we are more in tuned to our feelings and heart. However, I want to share this information so that it can help someone who needs it to heal their pain.

I lived with this woman and her family, thinking that her son was my father. As a child, our innocence allows us to follow adult figures and adhere to the demands that are given. I was told to call her "grandmother." At the ages of three and four years old, my "grandmother" at the time didn't have a bed or a room for me to stay in, so I slept in her and her husband's waterbed. The couple were probably in their early 40s. There were times in the middle of the night when I awoke in the bed to them having sexual relations. Even at four years old, I knew that this should not have been going on while I was in their bed. I remember wanting to get up out of the bed, but she would put her hand on my back to lay me back down. Of course, I didn't say anything to anyone because I was too young to truly understand what was happening. I just did as I was told and let it continue.

The following year was when the "grandmother" took it to the next level. She had introduced me to a man and said he was her brother. I am not sure if her husband had any clue about the brother or their relationship. I do remember family meals, and now I remember he was not present during the family gatherings. The only time I saw him was when the grandmother was by herself or at a friend's house. As an innocent child, I agreed and called him uncle. The next time that we met was with my "grandmother" at a motel close to the interstate. It was one of the cheap motels where people pay by the hour and meet to have sex.

It was a good day until we met up with him. The

"grandmother" took me out for breakfast and then to get a coloring book with crayons. Later, around lunch time, we went to the motel to meet her "brother." At the time, I thought it was very weird to meet her brother at a motel but, hey, what did I know? However, I knew something wasn't right when I saw them kissing on the lips, and I don't mean a peck on the lips, but you could see their tongues in each other's mouth. The feeling that I had was my internal spirit telling me that something bad was about to happen, something that was not supposed to happen. I honestly wish there was a picture of my face, because I'm sure I had a look as if I was about to throw up on them.

So, we went into one of the motel rooms. The "brother" had already gotten the key to open the door. As we went into the room, the "grandmother" told me to sit at a table with my back to the bed and color in my new coloring book. I remember my stomach ached when we walked into this room. The room smelled nasty and dirty. I didn't know at the time that Spirit was trying to warn me about what was to come.

The room was small with one bed, a nightstand, television, dresser, and one of those mirrors similar to what is in a convenience store, like the mirror above the door in the 7-11 where it looks like you weigh 30 more pounds than you actually do. The mirror was directly above my head.

As I began coloring, I heard moaning, and the bed was making noise. So, I looked in the mirror, curious about the noise. I saw them having sex. The thought that went through my head was, "No, you should not have sex with your brother!" Then I realized it couldn't be her brother and that this must be just some random guy. These are images that I can't erase from my mind. The smallest detail of him keeping his socks on has affected me all my life. Having been exposed to explicit sexual behavior as a child probably contributed to me engaging in sexual activity at a young age. I felt as though the only way I could be loved was through the act of sex.

As mothers, we must be aware that there are things we should not do around our children at any age. The children in this generation are exposed to sex on television, social media, and by peers at school. The lesson that I have learned from this experience is that sex is supposed to be a very private thing for a man and a woman.

Young women need to know — and believe — that they don't have to have sex to make a man love them; that is not what love is. Love, true love, is loving every aspect of a person, not just the sex: loving their laugh, blonde moments, being drunk, being mean, disagreeing, being selfish, and being there for each other during the hard times. This was the lesson I learned from the many relationships I've had during my lifetime. I view these life lessons as blessings; they helped me become the person I am today. I finally have the understanding that I am worthy of being loved for me and not for my body.

Shortly after the hotel experience, life returned to normal for about seven or eight months. I was almost six years old when the "brother" came back into the picture. We had gone over to the "grandmother's" friend's house for a barbeque. I was the only child there that day. So as any child would do, I played outside. Those were the good old days, no care in the world, using my imagination to create fairy tale stories while acting them out like I was in a Broadway show. For one moment, I imagined a happily-ever-after for myself, until there came the turning point that made me gasp for air because evil entered my life.

At almost six years old, while playing outside, all I wanted to do was to make mud pies. I had figured out the recipe for the perfect mud pie, and I needed more water. So, I grabbed a bucket and went to the bathroom inside the house. I was so excited! The feeling of accomplishment was my first taste of success. It is all about the small victories in life that truly make you feel blessed. As I stood at the sink filling my bucket of water, the "brother" came to the bathroom door.

He started with small talk: "What are you doing?"

"Making mud pies," I said.

"Oh, that sounds like fun." That was when the tone in his voice changed. I can still hear it to this day. His voice sounded an old man in a porn video who tries to sound sexy but ends up sounding like a pedophile who lives in the basement at his mom's house. He told me that once I was done filling the bucket, he had something to show me. Then he turned and left. I looked at myself in the mirror and said, "You are going to be okay, nothing is going to happen to you." This was a call from my heart for protection from my guardian angels. I had another weird feeling that something bad was getting ready to happen. Once again, Spirit tried to warn me that this was not going to be good.

As I came around the corner from the bathroom, I heard him call my name. I had hoped that I could just keep walking toward the door and go outside to continue my business of making mud pies. However, when I turned, there he was — sitting in the middle of the living room, butt naked, with his legs spread apart.

He said, "Come here. I want to show you something."

Looking at him, a feeling that was difficult for me to put into words at the time came over me. Today, I understand it was a feeling of nastiness and an understanding that this should not be happening. He told me to come closer to him. Then he said, "Let me see your hand." He grabbed my hand and made me touch his penis. I wanted to throw up.

He then said, "Come sit on my lap," and grabbed my hand, pulling me to sit on his lap.

Luckily, shortly after this happened, the "grandmother" started looking for me and calling for me. I ran out of the house, where I found her heading toward me. She asked, "What have you been doing in the house?" I told her that I was trying to make mud pies, which needed more water, and I also told her about her brother. She seemed mad at what she had heard. The grandmother pushed me aside as she ran in the house. I thought that she was going to protect me from that man. I knew in my gut I was right about how I was feeling when all this was going down. Always trust your gut! Always!

She ran into the house to talk to him about what I had just told her had happened. Several minutes passed. She came back outside and, as she was slapping me in the face, she told me that I should never lie about something like this. I told her that was the truth and that her brother was lying. No six-year-old child would lie about the details of a man or woman sexually abusing them. A child does not lie about sexual abuse from an adult; instead, a child is more likely to outline every detail about what happened to them.

At the time I thought, "Okay, if I tell what happens then I will be hurt or I will be in trouble for telling the truth." So, I started lying to her when things were happening around me. I said to myself, "If something else happens to me from this man, I am not going to tell her. I will find someone else to tell." I felt that was the only way I would be able to protect myself. This was my spiritual journey, and I was afraid to speak my truth, because I had been told by adults that my truth was a lie.

Soon afterwards, the "grandmother" was over at the "brother's" house making breakfast. She asked me to go wake him up. My stomach started hurting again as soon as she asked me to wake him up. In my heart, I knew he was going to be nasty again toward me. I knocked on his door and called for him to wake up for breakfast. It was dark in his room. I couldn't even see him while I stood in the doorway. No answer. So, I walked a little closer to his bed. He woke up and said, "Come get in the bed with me," as he lifted the covers to expose himself to me yet again. I simply said, "Breakfast is ready," and left his room. I remember going to bed that night praying that my mother or someone would come and save me from this home.

A few days later, my biological grandmother came to visit me. I was so grateful that my prayers had been answered. My real family had come to take me away from this horrible family. Her reappearance in my life was such a blessing because I was able to unburden myself and tell her everything that had happened. I knew when I saw her that this was going to be my way out of the nightmare I was living at that moment: the hotel, the mud pie, and the last breakfast.

Of course, social services got involved and contacted my biological mother to pick me up. I remember the day I left that house. I was so happy to be leaving that I would have left with anyone but the people living in that house. My biological mother stood at the front door and said, "I am your aunt, and I would like for you to come live with me. Would you like to come live with me?" I was so happy, I said, "Yes," and we were on our way. I am not sure why she called herself my aunt; it could have been the advice that social services gave her for fear that it would confuse me more than I already was as a child. It is also possible that her guilt got the best of her in that moment, and she felt that if she told me she was my aunt, I would not ask any questions about my mother. However, my mother did not think that through, because I made the connection that "aunt" means you are my mother's sister. "So where is my mother?"

That was the last time I ever saw that man or those people. Now was the time to start my mental and physical healing. Even though I have forgiven them for the trauma that I have faced, still, to this date, unfortunately, his face haunts me.

The "brother's" actions have affected me my whole life. I have tried so hard to block that experience from my mind. It is weird that small details of trauma affect a person's life and can make a person want to keep those details out of their life forever. I have been successful (most of the time) at blocking out the trauma of my childhood; however, there are days when I remember those dark times. The way I see it, those times were for me to reflect and heal the parts of my wounds that I have not yet healed.

This is a message for the children of the world: Do not be silent about any abuse. If the first person you tell doesn't listen to you, tell every person you meet until someone helps you. There are other victims of abuse who will listen and help you. You must always fight injustice that is occurring in your life in order to make a change. Only you are able to make a change in your life.

Once I had gotten comfortable with my new living situation, I was able to take a deep breath and actually be a child. For the next several weeks, I got so much love from my biological family. While living with her for the first couple of weeks, I still called her my aunt. Then the day came that she said, "I am not your aunt, I am actually your mother." I was then told by my biological mother that the man she was living with was my biological father. In my mind, at the age of six and a half, I had no idea as to what was actually happening in my life. We often lie to our children thinking that kids won't know the difference. That day, I didn't know what the hell to believe. I had no idea who I could trust and whose hands my life was in for the future. I never had a positive feeling about this man who was supposed to be my father. I wasn't sure if it was because of the recent trauma I had gone through or if he was simply not a good man.

He put on a mean front that was not comforting for a six-year-old who had been through so many traumas at the hands of a man. This man — my alleged father — made me feel like I was not supposed to be living with them. Like I was just another problem that had occurred in their lives. I am not sure if my mother wanted to believe that this man was my father or if she just told herself this for so many years that she actually believed it. But I never felt like he was my biological father. I didn't even look like him. At the time I was conceived, my mother had been with several different men. She had run away from home and was riding from truck to truck. To this day, I'm not sure who my father is.

In later years, my great grandmother told me that she believed that my father was a blond Swedish man who was a truck driver. These questions have haunted me my whole life:

"Who is my biological father?"

"What is he like?"

"Do I look like him?"

"Do I have brothers and sisters by this man?"

"Will I ever get the chance to meet him?"

Needless to say, I wasn't real fond of this man who she now claimed was my father.

I was blessed to have five consecutive generations of women in my family still alive. We all lived close together, which made getting together as a family easy and fun. Looking back, each of these women carried me in their womb and gave me a spiritual connection to my ancestors, who would help me along on my future spiritual journey.

I was able to get into a routine with my life. About a month after I moved back to Florida with my mother, I began to feel normal. I had not questioned her anymore regarding her reason for lying about being my mother. My heart was just happy to be around my family. It helped me feel normal knowing that I did have a family that I came from, my real family. All my worries seemed to disappear.

I often played outside with our dog, Sammy. Sammy was my buddy — we did so much together. He was a black Yorkshire dog. He would sleep with me at night. If my parents would horseplay with me, he bit their ankles.

My mother got me a bike and was teaching me how to ride it without training wheels. (One of the important lessons I learned from this is to always teach your children to ride a bike on a flat road, not a hill. The first time I tried to ride, I went down the driveway, which was on a long hill in front of our house. My mother forgot to show me where the brakes were on the bike. I ended up going really fast down the hill and ran into the gate at the end of the driveway. At that point, I decided to wait to try riding the bike again. Thank goodness there was a gate there to stop me, because I would have kept going right across the road into the ditch.)

There were some good memories during this time in my life. I remember getting my very first bed. We went to a furniture rental store to find the bed that I wanted. It was a red race-car bed. While we were in the store, I remember the sales associate saying usually boys are the ones who liked the race car beds. I told him that I liked to ride. I often dreamed of driving around the world.

My favorite memory was walking home from the bus stop after school to see my great-great grandmother, who had a large garden in her backyard. I remember coming home from school, and my granny would have a bowl of snap beans that she had picked out of the garden. We would drink a glass of sweet tea while we sat and talked about the school day. She would ask me things about what I had learned in school, how many friends I made that day, and what I hoped for the next day.

My great-great grandmother was a very loving woman who would do anything for someone in need. She would tell me stories of her life. She told me stories of losing family members and how it was hard to feed the family during the depression. Granny would also tell me that she was young when she started her family and share lessons of how she lived off the land. She said that this world has all the food in the world to end hunger if we could just recall our hunting and gathering skills from our ancestors. That woman was such a loving, beautiful, wise soul. I always looked forward to having those days with her and wished that they would never end.

Six months passed since I had started living with my biological mother. She was having trouble paying the rent for the house. We ended up moving to another county, because my "father" had gotten a job at a lumber yard operating a forklift. Some nights, while lying in bed, I overheard them arguing about how they were going to pay the bills. I believe that they were so far behind that they had received an eviction notice. So there went my happy moments with my great-great grandmother. Not to say that I didn't see her again. I did see her, I just did not get to share those special one-on-one moments with her every day.

A Mother's Wounded Heart

In 1992, my life was flipped upside down again. My mother and the man she was with were struggling financially to take care of me. We ended up moving to a trailer park in the next county. It was a big trailer with three bedrooms and two baths. My wardrobe consisted of a few outfits that I wore all week. I had play outfits, a school outfit, and a church dress. I did receive some clothes that my biological grandmother made for me as well. My biological mother wasn't working, so money was very tight. I remember having to wake up at 3:30 in the morning to go stand in the food stamp line just so we could get food for the month.

The one thing that I noticed about myself — not then, but now that I am an adult — was that I always was so grateful for the small things in life.

Because my parents at the time were having trouble paying rent, they decided to make a change. They knew a lady who needed to rent a room. She was nice and looked like a supermodel. Sometimes I would talk to her in the morning and watch her put makeup on. I would sit in the doorway, asking her questions about the makeup she used. I was so curious and wanted to try her makeup because I wanted to look pretty like she did.

At that time, I was being picked on at school because of my looks, and I thought that if I used her make-up I would look like her. Maybe then the kids would stop bullying me.

One day, I snuck into her room while she was not there and put some of her make-up on my face. It was just for five minutes and then I went to try to wash it off. I thought that I had put all the makeup back where I had gotten it from originally; however, I was caught by the lady who became so mad that she ended up moving out of the house.

Throughout my life, I have thought about the moment that woman left and recall a story my mother told me. She told me that my "father" loved young women. He was 10 years her senior. She said he was a big flirt with the young women, that he would jump at the chance if he could, if you know what I mean. I never caught him cheating, but I have a feeling that was what happened.

When this occurred, my biological mother asked me if I had gone into the lady's room and put makeup on my face… while she could still see some of it on my face. I looked her in the eye and said, "No." I lied because I didn't want to get in trouble for telling the truth. I was protecting myself. I had already experienced what happens when I told the truth, and I didn't want that to happen again. This was how I tried to protect myself. I didn't trust her; I hardly knew her as my mother.

My birthday was going to be the next day, and I knew it wasn't going to be a good birthday for me since I had gotten in trouble for lying. At that age, I very much loved "The Little Mermaid" by Disney. I wanted a stuffed animal of Flounder, the yellow and blue fish from the movie. My biological mother had gone out and gotten me Little Mermaid toys for my birthday gifts, but because I had gotten in trouble for lying to her about the makeup, she took them all back to the store. Of course, not before she showed me what she had gotten me for my birthday. Happy sixth birthday! You get nothing! I couldn't believe that she would take away my birthday gifts all because I made a mistake. As I cried in my room, reflecting on my behavior, I asked for better days.

In the trailer park where we lived, a bus would come around and take kids to church on Sunday morning. Oh, it was so exciting to go to church. I loved going to church. I was the only one in my family who went to church. I would often ask my parents to go with me, but the father was working, and my mom didn't have transportation.

Church made my heart and soul feel so amazing. I would wake up early, eat breakfast, get dressed, and go to bible study then to church. It was as if I was feeding my heart and soul to hear about Jesus and the many things he had done to help people. All the hope that was placed in people's heart if they only followed his words. There were times when I was sitting in church and the Holy

Spirit would touch my heart, even though I had no idea what I was feeling. It was amazing for me to experience that at such an early age. I knew then that God would always keep his children close to his heart. Every time I heard the worship music, with songs such as "Amazing Grace," I had goosebumps and sometimes tears. At the time, I was not aware that the goosebumps were a sign of Spirit in my soul speaking to me. I didn't know that the Holy Spirit was speaking to my wounded heart.

One Sunday the pastor asked, "Is there was anyone who wants to be saved and baptized?" I jumped up and said, "I do!" The congregation got loud with excitement that a child so young understood and wanted to receive Jesus. They all were clapping and expressing joy for me. The pastor yelled, "Hallelujah! Thank you, Jesus, for this child. Let her be an example for others."

I wanted Jesus in my life because I felt as though the people in my life had no clue what they were doing. I wanted his protection because of the things that had happened to me in the past. That was the day my spiritual journey started with Jesus. I was so happy when I came home from church that Sunday. When I got home, I told my mother how my day was and that I had accepted Jesus as my savior. She shared a hug and kiss on the forehead and said she loved me. "I always knew you were so special," she said.

A sense of peace and forgiveness came over my heart like fresh water on a beach. I felt that my innocence had been returned to me by the healing power of the words from Jesus. The seed of the Holy Spirit and Jesus had been planted in my heart and was waiting to grow with every piece of knowledge I could learn about God. Just as Jesus had his time to walk and be tested by evil, I had no idea then that the direction of my life would drive a wedge between me and my relationship with God.

When we lived in the trailer park, I tried to make friends with the neighborhood kids. The kids were so mean to me, though. My teeth were messed up with a big gap in front. I had warts on my elbows and fingers. There was a time that I remember talking back to my mother. She pushed me, which caused me to fall on the floor across a metal strip, resulting in the warts being cut open. My hair wasn't kept up, and I didn't have new or trendy clothes. Since the kids were bullying me at the bus stop every afternoon, I started developing my fight-or-flight instincts. I was so tired of being bullied and was going to stand in my truth.

One day, coming home from school on the bus, the kids were brutal toward me. I remember not saying one damn word to anyone; I just sat there, glaring at them. They said, "When we get off the bus, let's beat the ugly out of her." I was so mad that these kids were messing with me. I just wanted it to stop. So, I made the decision that I was going to kick that boy in his balls for saying that to me. It was not the best decision, because after I kicked the kid, all the other kids at the bus stop grabbed sticks and started hitting me and beating me upside the head with them. I was so mad that this boy, who I didn't know or play with, would say something like that. I didn't say his face looked like a donkey's ass. No. I was trying to make friends so I wouldn't feel so lonely. I came home that day with bruises all over my body from being hit by sticks.

My "father" (so she said) was so mad that I had kicked this kid in the balls. He grabbed me by my arms and said, "You never kick someone in their private parts. If you want to hit someone, you hit me. Hit me! Hit me!" I didn't want to do it. He was my "father," and it wasn't right to hit him. He wouldn't stop saying "hit me" until I hit him. I felt like I was the worst person in the world for defending myself and kicking that boy in his private area then having to hit "my father" in the face.

He then instructed me to go outside to a bush that had branches with thorns and bring a branch to him. I was spanked with the branch on my butt as punishment. It says in the bible to honor thy mother and father, but how do you honor a person who causes you pain? I tried to explain to them that the kids were bullying me and that they beat me up at the bus stop; however, they didn't want to hear what I had to say. This was another lesson learned: don't hit someone just because of what they say to you. Don't allow anger to cloud your judgement.

Not long after that day of having my self-esteem broken down by these kids, my mother came to me with news that would change my direction in life yet again. She informed me that I was going to live with my cousin in Virginia. It was a complete surprise to me when my mother said that I was going to live in Virginia. I didn't understand why I had to go through this again. I'd never been to Virginia and had no idea where it was on the map. "God, why is this happening again?" I asked. "When will someone love me?" My heart was broken all over again.

There were so many different questions going through my head.

Why are you giving me up again?
What have I done wrong for you not to want me?
What is this family like?
Is it going to be like the other family?
Is this permanent or temporary?

I had so much anger, pain, feelings of unworthiness, and sadness. I was broken inside. Once again, I felt as though I was never going to be loved. I would often ask myself, "Why am I alive if no one wants me?" That night, I cried myself to sleep asking God to prevent this from happening.

The first time I talked to my cousin, I was very nervous. I had already been betrayed and abandoned twice by the person who was supposed to protect me. My mother was the one person who was supposed to love me unconditionally for my ugly face, my bad behavior, and my crazy soul. When I answered the phone, I was happy to hear her voice was nice; it was calm. My cousin asked, "Would you like to come live in Virginia?"

I was so angry with my biological mother that she would do this to me again. "Yes," I said. Then something occurred to me. "Is this temporary?" I asked. "Can I bring my cat, Charlie?" I was done playing the back-and-forth game with this person (aka my mother) who claimed that she was going to take care of me when I first met her. If she didn't want me, then I didn't want her in my life.

My cousin and her mother — who was my biological great-great-aunt — drove from Virginia to Florida to pick me up. On the day that my cousin (soon to be my new mom) and her mother (soon to be my new grandma) arrived, I packed my clothes, my cat Charlie, and his food. Charlie was the one constant I had in life. I had saved him from the side of the road. It is very ironic that, at the age of seven, as I was being given to another family, I was saving another life that had been abandoned by his only mother. My mother was very quiet that day, and she sat in the living room watching for them to arrive. As we sat together for what I thought was going to be the last time, I asked, "Why can't I live with my uncle who has horses?" This uncle was my biological grandmother's brother. He had horses and was often in rodeo tournaments. I loved going to see him and watching him ride his horses.

"That is where I want to live," I said to my mother.

"I asked if he could take you, and unfortunately he cannot," she stated.

My new mom asked me, "Do you have everything that you want to take with you?"

"Yes, I do."

She said, "You are more than welcome to call me by my name, or you can call me mom." I looked at my biological mother for what I thought would be the last time, then turned to my new mom and said, "I will call you Mom!" We grabbed my things, loaded the car, and started our journey to my new home in Virginia.

Chapter 2
New Beginnings

Arriving in Virginia in 1992 marked a fresh start for me. I got a new home, new family, new name, and a new life. Honestly, it felt like God had just poured so much love over me by taking me away from a life that was so painful. It takes a selfless person or persons to take in a damaged child whose soul was so broken and nurture them to be the best person they can be in life.

I am forever grateful for my new parents. The first day that we arrived in Virginia, I was in awe of how beautiful the county was in which we lived. The small town was surrounded by water. The house was a brick rancher with a detached garage. It had a fenced-in backyard. My new grandmother lived in the same small town that we did, and she was only about ten minutes away. When we pulled up to the house, my new dad was standing in the garage and, as soon as we pulled up, I ran to him with a big hug, calling him daddy. To this day, he still tells people that was the moment I stole his heart.

When I saw this new house, I knew I had a new life. I didn't know anyone there except for my new mom and new grandmother. I went into the house with my cat and my suitcase, and I was introduced to my new brothers. My older brother is an outdoorsman. He was coming in the door from hunting in the woods across the street, I believe. The younger of the two brothers was in the house when I came through the door. This was awesome that I was going to have such a big family now. My mom said, "Come, I will show you where your room is." I couldn't believe all the nice things they had in the house. In my heart, I was saying, "I can't believe that this is happening to me." I was still kind of in shock about everything that had happened that week.

The room was beautiful, with a rocking chair, a twin bed with blue and pink flowered bedding, two dolls that had been my new mom's childhood toys, and a heart-shaped hook rug that my biological great-great-grandmother had made for me. It was very interesting to me that, by agreeing to live in Virginia, I felt that I was on another spiritual journey. When I saw that room, I could feel God saying, "Here is your new life. You have everything you need right here. You have parents who are going to love you, you have two brothers to pick on you and joke with you, and you have your cat!" When my new mom asked me what I thought of my room, I said, "I think this will work," like I was some kind of big shot with executive power or something.

I often wonder what my mom was feeling when she made this decision to open her home to me. She was aware of the history of my past life. Of course, there was no question whether or not to take me into her home. It took about three days for me to realize all that had happened with my biological mother. Soon after arriving in Virginia, I started questioning my mom about the events in my life. *What was the plan for the future? Would I ever live with my biological mother again? Would I ever see her again? Why did she give me up twice to different people?* I asked my mom these questions all the time.

In response, she shared the stories that she had heard over the years about me. The story that was going around the family was that my biological mother had run away from home and gotten pregnant by a truck driver. In fact, my new parents had tried to adopt me when I was a baby and were told by the family that other arrangements had already been made. This was the last thing that was told to my new parents. There was a lot of miscommunication, shame and lies that involved this experience in my life.

My great grandmother had told my new mom, "We take care of our own around here." I believe that is why my new mom did pursue adoption after that because of the shame that my biological family had about my situation. With that being said, I have always struggled with trusting people.

My mind started racing again, wondering if I could actually be happy. In the past, I had gotten my hopes up to be able to have something good with my biological mother. What if my life turned out to be miserable with this new family? I was searching for the good with my new family, new home, and new life, while trying to get the truth about my life story. My fear and lack of trust in people made it difficult to let a new family into my heart; however, with their love, they eventually helped me trust again. I rode my emotions like a damn rollercoaster. Some days I cried myself to sleep, and some days I didn't have a care in the world.

My childhood trauma caused me to question every aspect of my life, an unfortunate habit that has bled into my adult life. Even today, I have trouble letting people into my life.

During the first couple of weeks, my mom took me shopping for clothes, to get a haircut, and to the doctor for a health checkup. I was taken to several different doctors: the primary care doctor, the wart doctor, and then the dentist. Each doctor's visit was a scary experience, because I could not remember going to a doctor before. At my primary care doctor visit, I had to get current on the immunizations for school. I sat on my mom's lap and screamed at the top of my lungs. My mom said it was a high-pitched, screeching sound. She said, "If you get these shots, I will take you shoe shopping!" What girl who didn't ever have much wouldn't want to go shoe shopping? I immediately stopped screaming and got the shots. My mom laughs when she shares that story and says her ears still ring! This was one of many great memories that marked the beginning of my new life journey.

My parents were members of the Catholic church in our town. My grandparents and parents went to church every Sunday. When I was in Florida, I had been going to a Baptist church. I was not familiar with the Catholic religion. It was a hard transition into the Catholic religion for me because I had been taught that your relationship is with Jesus alone and that you confess your sins to Jesus and no one else. However, in the Catholic religion, confession is done directly with the priest. You repent your sins and pray for forgiveness all within the confines of the confessional box. Even though I was not a believer in confessing my sins to the priest, I converted to the Catholic religion as a child in order to continue my spiritual journey with Jesus. I knew that I would still receive my messages from him even though it was a different way to worship. There were times when we went to mass, and it felt as though the priest was talking directly to me, but it was really just Jesus or God making sure I had the messages I needed for the week.

I started second grade in a new school. As a child, I had trouble making friends. I always thought it was because of the way I looked. Since moving to Virginia, however, my appearance started to change. I had so many clothes that I had to pick my clothes out the night before. I was one of those girls who would try five different outfits on to make sure I felt comfortable in the clothing before I left the house. This process was to decide if the clothes made me feel pretty. The warts were going away, I had braces to fix my teeth, and I had a great new haircut. My self-esteem was still broken because of the kids in Florida; however, I was able to make a few friends I could possibly hang out with.

I became friends with a couple of kids who lived behind me in the neighborhood, and we played together almost every weekend. We had so much fun. We built a fort in the backyard and used our imagination to create stories. In the summer, we stayed out until 10p.m., playing kick-the-can and flashlight tag. These were the good memories, ones that every child should have. Kids should be free from experiencing adult drama.

When I arrived in Virginia, my mom and dad started the process of adopting me. I had no idea that my adoption was going to take two years to be granted. Apparently, the delay was caused by my biological mother, who would not come to Virginia to sign the papers. So my parents had to put an announcement in the local newspaper as well as a newspaper in the state where my biological mother lived to confirm that there was no one to contest the adoption. I asked my mom every day if the adoption was complete until the day of the court hearing. It was a very happy day for me. It was an awesome feeling for the adoption to be complete and it was official: I had a new identity and a new permanent home.

But my happiness was short lived. The truth is that kids like me, with a trauma-based background, have a difficult time adjusting and coping to a new reality.

Having a new home and new parents did not mean that my life was magically perfect. Since coming to Virginia, I struggled with depression. I didn't know at that time what depression was or how to describe what I was feeling. My behavior worsened, and I was in trouble all the time. When I was told to do something or if I had disobeyed, I would definitely voice my opinion on the matter. I felt as though my opinion should be heard. It was my life, not theirs.

Because I was often grounded to my room, I went back

to feelings of isolation again. I was always sad. This was the time where I would reflect and talk to God the most. It is interesting that when we feel our worst, we are quick to call upon him to save us, yet we fail to talk to him when all is well. At times, my parents would tell the therapist that they could not understand why I was misbehaving, and they would communicate their disapproval as if I was the most terrible person in the world. The therapist told me that the reason I was depressed was because of all the tragedy that had occurred in my life up to the age of seven years old. I had a deep well of anger that I could not let go of, especially related to my biological mother giving me up.

My biological mother called my new mom and told her that she would be driving through Virginia and asked if she could stop by for a visit. Reluctantly, my new mother agreed to do dinner. She was nervous about how this visit was going to turn out. We had been making progress, and she was afraid that this was going to move us backwards in the healing process.

When my biological mother arrived, she came with the man she had claimed was my father. By the end of dinner, she had gotten me so upset at the fact that she was leaving me here in Virginia that my parents had to ask her to leave so I could get ready for bed. Again, my younger self faced an emotional rollercoaster. Despite the pain she had brought to me, I wanted to leave with her. My biological mother said they were making money now. It wasn't logical, but I wanted to be with someone who had my blood. I wanted my mother. I was angry that she came to Virginia just to say goodbye again. What the fuck was the point? Did she enjoy seeing me in pain? She knew all I wanted in life was her; I wanted her love. My heart couldn't take any more of her bullshit, talking and trying to explain. None of her actions made sense to me. She was wasting my time and hers.

Even though it didn't make sense to an outsider, I longed to be with her. I wanted her approval more than anything in life. The next time I saw my biological mother was when I was fourteen at my great-great grandmother's funeral.

Parents should always support their children's dreams and the desires of their heart. There were times in my life that people would have something negative to say about an idea I had for my future. I have found this a very difficult lesson to learn in the sense of hearing non-supportive feedback from people who I thought were on my side. Society is completely engrossed with the idea of having a job in a field that will provide for the family. The overwhelming concern is what career is going to provide the most financial stability which, unfortunately, can cause people to forget the desires of their heart. The universe is always going to provide abundance as long as you do what is in your heart. I dreaded having a career that drained the life out of my soul every time I walked in. I have learned to take what people say with a grain of salt simply because I always had a feeling that I had a higher purpose in life. I know that God has a great plan for me, and don't ever doubt there is a great plan in place for you, too.

Years later, I learned that my family is predisposed to depression and suicide. My new parents took me to the doctor who prescribed antidepressants for me. The doctor had also prescribed Ritalin and labeled me as having ADD (attention deficit disorder). He told me the medicine would help me focus in school.

Some of the medication made my depression worse, to the point where I was cutting myself to let the pain out, and some made me so happy that it was too much. At the end of the day, I didn't want to be on medication for depression, because it made me numb to everything in life. Don't get me wrong, I wanted to be numb from the pain that I had already endured. I just wanted that pain to go away so I could feel normal, like all my friends. During my dark emotional and mental battles during my adolescence, my behavior worsened.

My reasons for cutting were deep-seated, but as I said, I did it to release my inner pain. My behavior spiraled out of control because I felt that I should be able to do whatever I wanted and should not have to answer to anyone. This, in turn, made my life a living hell and my family's life miserable. I simply could not heal from the pain of my childhood. It was a bug bite I kept scratching, but it got worse and became infected because I could not get closure on the situation. I acted out against the people who loved me. I figured if I misbehaved enough, they would give me up like my biological mother did, and I would get a new life.

This was a very dark chapter in my life, and I lost my path on my spiritual journey. I stopped talking to God; I didn't want to have anything to do with him or hear what he was trying to say to my heart. Looking back, I realize that I had to go through that dark chapter to prepare for the next hand that was dealt to me.

As a teenager, I thought that in order to be loved, a person had to have sex. This confusion was a result of my childhood experiences. Puberty started much earlier for me than my classmates. My parents knew that this was going to be an issue. They wanted to make sure that I was not going to get pregnant as a teenager like my biological mother did at the age of 15. I was interested in boys and continuously pursued them, even at the age of 10.

A Mother's Wounded Heart

My adoptive mother and I didn't have a best-friend relationship. As a child, I was hard-headed, wanted to do what I wanted, and felt I didn't have to answer to anyone. Because of my past trauma, there was a lack of trust on my part with anyone who was introduced in my life. I questioned why I had to listen to my adoptive parents or any authority figures. Everyone felt that they knew what was best for me, including the damn doctors, therapist, and so on. Most people who tried to help me made one big mistake: they failed to realize that I was on my own journey.

I always thought that true love comes from your mother. This is not just for your biological mother; this is for foster parents and adoptive parents as well. A word of advice for adoptive parents, or foster parents: it doesn't help a child's self-esteem if you introduce them as your foster child or adopted child. It made me feel as though I was a charity case or that I didn't belong with the family. The behavior that I displayed as a child caused a big wedge between me and the family who was trying to love me unconditionally.

My adoptive mother had so much frustration toward me, and I had the same toward her. I recently had a conversation with my new mom and told her, "I never felt you gave me unconditional love." My mother replied, "I associate love with trust." *So you never truly loved me unconditionally because you didn't trust me*, I thought. That statement really put things into perspective for me, because I was able to see how my mother truly felt about the lack of trust that I placed in her heart. The pain that I caused on her heart because I couldn't trust her.

It was hard for me to tell my adoptive mother how I truly felt while growing up. It was so painful that I have tried to block that out in my life; however, I have learned that if you don't deal with negative life experiences, they will continue to eat at your soul. The trauma I suffered made living very difficult for me and eventually caused me to completely shut down. There was no way I was going to talk to my mom about my day or the day I had my first kiss in school. As a child, I was confused and torn, and I never felt like she was my mom; however, since I have grown and had my own children, she is my mother, and we are now able to have a best-friend relationship in our lives.

My adoptive parents made sure I had counseling for years, trying to help me deal with the depression that I suffered from because of the sexual, mental, and physical abuse I had endured. I have to be honest; I never felt that it helped me to tell someone I didn't know what was going on in my head. They had no idea what I had gone through or the feelings that came from dealing with it.

I hope this book provides some kind of insight that

people can relate to or to just know that they are not the only ones who have been through this trauma. At that moment in my life, I only wanted to know why all this happened to me without recognizing that this was about my spiritual journey.

I'm sure every parent has felt that there were things they could have done differently while raising their children. The times have changed when it comes to raising child. Parents need to simply love their children unconditionally; even when children are acting out or lying, be sure to tell them you love them no matter what.

Children need to know they are loved. When a child gets in trouble, they immediately assume that their parent, or parents, don't love them anymore. As a child, I would get in trouble and this same feeling would arise. I would say I was sorry and that I loved them. The reply was, "Thank you for your apology. Goodnight." There were times where I did hear, "I love you;" however, I was in trouble more than I was good. The lack of love that was expressed left me feeling like a piece of shit; it never helped my self-esteem. My give-a-fuck was broken. I didn't care anymore whether people loved me or not.

I now have two healthy and handsome boys. I discipline them when they are in trouble, but I always tell them I love them. Always. I never heard "I love you" every day. My children and I never go to bed without giving each other a hug, kiss, and saying I love you. I started this trend when my children were just starting to walk and talk. I never felt loved, so I made a promise to the Universe, my future children, and myself that I would always love and fight for them.

I used to tell my children, "You are stuck with me."

One day my oldest told me, "You are stuck with me forever."

From the ages of 13 to 16, I was very concerned with my appearance. I would not eat because I felt as though I was fat. The summer before going into sixth grade, I gained a lot of weight. I was eating a lot because I was lonely, having to stay at the house all by myself. I wasn't allowed to play with my friends until my dad got home from work. My mom had to take me shopping because none of my clothes fit me due to the weight gain. I figured I could fix this problem by not eating.

My parents were concerned with the fact that I had stopped eating. They took me to the doctor and, of course, the doctor stated that if I didn't eat, then he was going to have to give me a feeding tube. I felt as though I wasn't doing anything wrong by not eating. I had lost all the extra weight and fit into my old clothes. Because of this, my mother didn't have to buy me new clothes. These thoughts stayed in my head because I was afraid to speak my truth. The doctor diagnosed me as severely depressed and determined that was why I was not eating. In retrospect, I was trying to heal my self-esteem by losing weight.

My parents were extremely concerned about so much of what was happening in my life: depression, not eating, cutting myself, and threatening suicide. Because of this, they listened to the doctor's suggestion to send me to a behavioral center. This was the first time that I had ever interacted with people with true mental diseases. This was a very shocking experience, yet I was enlightened by the information that I received in the center. I was angry at my parents for sending me to what I called a mental institution. Questions rolled through my mind. *Why am I being put in this place? I do not have a mental disease.* I just had so much pain, but instead of helping, I believe that place did more damage than good for me.

I shared a room with a girl who was so depressed and had anxiety so bad that she pulled her hair out. At night, I laid awake in fear while screams echoed through the hospital. During those times, I talked to God. I asked him to take me away from this world. I told him that I didn't want to live in this world anymore because the pain was too hard for me to bear. I could not understand why God would have me suffer through all these experiences in life. God is a merciful God, he doesn't want people to suffer pain, loss, fear, depression, or grief. I became so angry with God that I stopped talking to him. The age of 18, which would liberate me, couldn't come fast enough.

I was in a behavioral center over one Christmas holiday. Later, my parents told me that was the most peaceful holiday they'd had since I came to live with them. It was difficult for me to understand why I was in this center for not eating. It seemed obvious to me back then that I was not supposed to be in there with these people who were in worse condition than me. Placing me in this facility generated the same feelings of abandonment that my biological mother had created. I couldn't understand why I was being subjected to this mental trauma at the age of 15. I just wanted to be able to be me, and my parents didn't understand why I was displaying this behavior. What they didn't know was that this was my way of coping with the pain in my wounded heart.

The age of 16 was rough for me only because I had made up my mind that I knew everything about being an adult. There were times in my teenage years where I would run away, and I would always hope to get farther than the last time. I would go to a friend's house, the woods, and to another state. This was the same behavior that my biological mother displays.

I hope and pray every day that my children don't feel the need to run away from me. I was so tired of being controlled by my parents. I had been lying to them for so many years that they didn't trust me at all. Because my parents couldn't trust me, I was often on lockdown. I was so tired of not being able to do what I wanted to do that I made up my mind to run away. I wanted to be a teenager who has the ability to spend the night at a girlfriend's house. To be able to go on a date with my boyfriend. To be free to find out who I was and make my own decisions. This was not the best idea that I had; however, at the time it sounded logical to my young self.

My parents gave me a car to use for school and work. I did okay with that privilege for a while. I took the car that my parents allowed me to use and called my so-called biological father to come pick me up. My parents were so tired of the lies and the disrespect that I had been showing them. Plus, my grandmother had been diagnosed with lung cancer, so my parents were under a lot of stress and should not have had to deal with my behavior. My mother took this as a personal attack against her while she was dealing with her mother dying. I just wanted to get away from that family; I didn't feel wanted so I figured I would leave them alone as they had done to me. Problem solved, right? No, it only made things so much worse.

My parents contacted the police to file a report of me running away with the car. I was charged with grand larceny. The courts sent me to the local detention center to serve my sentence. In my mind, I railed at the knowledge that parents are supposed to nurture their child, love them even when they are doing something wrong. This was not love to me; instead, I felt attacked by the people who claimed they loved me. I was in flight or fight mode. I just wanted to get away from Virginia. It became crystal clear to me at that point that my parents would go to whatever extremes necessary to make sure I learned my lesson. Some extremes were unnecessary, to my way of thinking, such as charging their child with grand larceny. That could have given me a felony on my criminal record, which would have kept me from having a good career. I have not been in trouble with the law since then except for a speeding ticket.

The weird part of being in the detention center was that I felt as though I shouldn't have been in there. Again, I was nothing like the other kids serving their time for bigger crimes than I would have ever considered committing. While I was in the detention center, I had told the judge that I was being mentally abused by my parents. There were kids in there who had killed their parents. Some of the kids were in there for fighting with people. There were kids in there for drugs. While I was in the detention center, I told some lies about my parents to the court.

For example, the last time that I had run away I had gone to my boyfriend's neighborhood, where the police found me. They brought me home to my parents. My mother was livid about the clothes I was wearing. I had borrowed some of my boyfriend's clothes because my clothes had gotten wet. When I got home, my mother took me into the bathroom, stood in the doorway, and made me take my clothes off. As I stood in front of her, naked, my heart felt as though it was going to jump right out of my chest in fear of her being even more angry with me. She made me turn around because she saw something on my hip. It was a tattoo of a butterfly that I had gotten the year before when I ran away. My mother called my dad, my brother, and the police officer who brought me home and made them look at me naked. I do not remember if the police officer or my brother came over to look, but I held my head down in shame once my self- esteem was gone.

I was humiliated. How dare she do that to me in front of three men? Her actions catapulted me back to my childhood, and that wound was split wide open again. All the work I had done to heal that part of my life, and now the wound split open again, deeper. I was done with this family. I couldn't take any more trauma from them, so I told the court I didn't want to return to their home.

The local county had a program that was similar to a temporary foster home where I could live until I turned 18. I lived with a woman in a town about 30 minutes from my parents. Once again, I started at a new school and in a new home. It was amazing to have the ability to not live at that house. I even went by my middle name in the new school. I had more friends in this high school. I did, however, miss my boyfriend. He loved me to the moon and back. He would leave school and come see me at a little country convenience store where I worked. My boyfriend was quiet and kind, the type of boy who would do anything for you. I was his first everything. We met in school where he sat alone, eating. We got to know each other, and the next thing I knew, we were inseparable.

Like any teenager filled with angst over being separated from her boyfriend, I ended up running away from the foster home to be with him. Because of that action, I was sent back to the detention center to finish serving my time until I was 18 years of age.

In the detention center, I learned so much. I learned that as someone who was getting ready to turn 18, if the court system sentences you to the detention center at 17, you still have to serve your sentence until your 18th birthday and, if not, they could transfer you to the regional jail. I didn't want to start my adult life in jail.

The second time in the detention center, with the help

of the staff, I was able to regain focus on what it was that I wanted in life. I reconnected with God. For the longest time, I couldn't understand why He allowed all these things to happen to me, not realizing it was my decisions that placed me in these life situations. He is always teaching me a lesson. Every day, we have lessons from Him. There are times when we must experience these lessons more than once. I was a person who had to experience it more than one time.

One of the four ladies who worked in the detention center told me, "You will be great one day! God has a plan for you!" This really helped my self-esteem. Nobody had ever said that to me. Instead, my parents used to tell me if I didn't graduate high school I would end up working at McDonald's, asking the customer if they would like fries with that burger. This is not support. This pissed me off when my parents said this to me, and I heard it a lot during my time in high school.

I knew deep in my heart that I was going to amount to something. That I was here for a reason, whether they believed it or not. I used to imagine the looks on their faces when I achieved my life's purpose. My spirit moved for a moment in my heart then, and there was hope again for something more. I was very well behaved, and a lot of the staff felt I shouldn't have been in that center.

I have hurt so many people in my life, and they have

hurt me. I hope they can forgive me one day.

When I turned eighteen in March, my mom picked me up from the detention center. I hadn't seen her much since September. I didn't know what to say to the family. I am sure that they wanted an explanation for all the pain I had caused them. There wasn't a lot that was said between me and my mom except that she had re-enrolled me in school. She did ask what I wanted to do for my birthday. Of course, I told her I wanted to see my friends and boyfriend.

When I left the house to meet my friends, the agreement was that I would return home by 8:30. I called my mom and told her that I was spending the night with a friend. My boyfriend and I went out to eat and then returned to his neighborhood. I was 18 and free. It was the best feeling; finally, freedom. I didn't have to answer to anyone but myself.

I had a blast that night. We listened to music until the morning hours, laughed, and played games. I didn't go home, and they didn't know where I was for a while.

When I called home to let my parents know that I was okay and still alive, my mother answered the phone and told me that my stuff was on the front porch. I didn't believe her. I had no idea she was serious. I asked my boyfriend to drive past the house to see if that was the truth. Sure enough, my stuff was packed and sitting on the front porch. I said to myself, "Fine, I got this." I walked up to the front porch, grabbed my bags, and left, never wanting to see them ever again. My parents had packed only a few pairs of jeans, a couple of shirts, underwear, and a pair of shoes in the original suitcase that I had arrived with from Florida.

They were finished with all my bullshit. I had done so much damage with my lies and behavior that they felt as though there was nothing more they could do for me. I only had three months left before graduating from high school. I made the decision to stay out, which then led to me being homeless.

This was my true reality check.

I was 18, and I had no food, no money, nowhere to live, and nowhere to shower. The next hurdle was to find a job. For a few weeks, I stayed in an abandoned house in the woods near where my boyfriend lived. This house sat at the entrance into his neighborhood. It was a two-story house, similar in style to a colonial house. Windows were busted out and tree limbs had fallen around the yard. When I first walked in the house, it was obvious that someone had been living there recently. The floor was littered with trash. My boyfriend got me a few things from his house: blankets, pillow, and a flashlight so I could see to do my homework. I was scared that whoever had recently been staying at this abandoned house was going to come back while I was there. My boyfriend did sneak out of his house some nights to come stay with me, so in those moments I felt safe. He was my rock; I was very much in love with him. I would get up in the morning, go to his house to take a shower, and walk to the bus stop to go to school. We would time the shower to happen after his dad left and before his mom woke up. They had no idea this was going on in their house.

These living conditions were not healthy for me, but I was doing my best to get my diploma. My situation was far from ideal, and I couldn't stand living in that abandoned house. I thought, "I need to go back to Florida. I have a place I can stay down there." I thought I could stay with my biological mother. So, I dropped out of school and went to Florida in search of her.

I had an address book that listed my biological grandmother's phone number and address. My boyfriend paid for my bus ticket to Florida, and my grandmother had my biological mother pick me up from the bus station. I was on an emotional high. I was so excited to be leaving Virginia and going home. Eighteen years old, riding a bus with strangers, praying that nothing happened to me on the way down to Florida.

When we pulled in to the bus station, I spotted her outside. She was crying, I was crying. I had missed her so much. All the anger that I held toward her was nowhere to be found. She hugged me so tight and grabbed my face. "You are so beautiful," she said.

This is it, I thought. *All those questions that I have been waiting for the answer to are now here in front of me.*

However, I didn't have the courage to ask her any questions out of fear of the pain I would have to revisit for myself and her. At that time, she was not with the man who she had told me was my father. She was with a man from Idaho. When we got to her car, a baby was in the back seat. "Who is that?" I asked.

"It's my baby, your little brother," she said.

I was shocked. My mother had a son. I had a half-brother who was 18 years younger than me! I was so desperate to have that relationship that I had yearned for my whole life. This was both a sad and happy moment for me at the time: Happy that I had a little brother, very sad to see her taking care of him when she hadn't been able to take care of me as a child. I promised that I was always going to be there for him.

My mother always had bad taste in men. At that time, she was with another troubled man who abused her. When I first met him, I wanted to punch him in the face.

There was a time when she called me; he had given her a black eye. I asked, "How can I help? You need to leave. What can I do?" She didn't want to leave him, and I didn't understand why she would let this man abuse her.

I got angry with her and told her, "I don't know what you want me to do for you." At this time in my life, I really was not able to help her, but I was going to do whatever it took for her to leave him once she had decided. Years later, I discovered that he had threatened to kill her and her son if she left him, and she believed he would.

I ended up riding with her to Georgia, where she was trying to get a long-haul trucking job. I rode with her to her interview with this new company. I ended up meeting a man who was infatuated with me. He was a nice man but wanted me to marry him right then and there, even though I had just met him.

We had a great weekend together; he took me on romantic dates that weekend. We partied with his friends, but he wanted me to stay with him and start a life. My mother hadn't heard from me in a few days, so she showed up at his door. She stood at the door, knocking until I answered. I felt ashamed to be up in the house of an older man. It was almost like I was 16 again.

"Come talk to me for a minute," she said. When I stepped outside, she asked, "Why didn't you answer the door when you heard me call for you?"

"I thought you she would be mad… disappointed that I was in his house because he is eight years older than me."

She looked at me and said, "Tina Marie, you are 18 years old. I am not going to tell you what to do."

No judgement — that was a relief. However, I knew leading this man on wasn't right, because I was not going to marry him or stay in Georgia. I had only been in Georgia for three days, and I was ready to come back to Virginia. I told the man that I had to finish school in Virginia, and I would return to him when I was done. Just another lie, right? It was me not speaking my truth for fear of upsetting someone.

Shortly after, I returned to Virginia to start my adult life with no high school diploma.

After coming home to Virginia, I resumed sleeping in the abandoned house. My mother had given me some money so I could buy food and hygienic items until I could get a job. But this lifestyle was not sustainable, and I needed money. A friend who lived in that neighborhood told me I could be a stripper. The idea of making good money without needing a high school diploma appealed to me. I ended up getting a job as a stripper, hoping to make enough money to be able to buy food and have a place to live.

Deciding to pursue this was not easy. I knew this was not what I was meant to do in my life. I had completely turned my back on God and on my spiritual journey. I had lost my sense of self-worth once again.

This was the first couple of months of my adulthood. As I look back on this turning point in my life, I wish I had made better decisions.

The strip club gave me a job. My first night, I was so scared to get up on that stage and dance. It was me and a woman with one arm on stage. I told her that I had never done anything like this before in my life. She said, "Before you go out there, watch me and see how I do it, then create your own style." She worked that pole with one arm like a professional. "Man, if only I could be like that, I could make good money," I thought. In high school, I had been on the flag team, so I had already danced in front of a lot of people. The only difference was that now I had a lot less clothes on. The image of my body was perfect. White girl, fair skin, curved in all the right places, and a fat ass. That was the first time I was truly confident in my self-image. I knew I looked good, because I wasn't eating and there wasn't any fat on my body.

It wasn't a busy strip club. The first night I worked, I only made 50 dollars. Thank goodness I made some money to get food and items I needed. At that point, I still didn't have a car or a place to live. The owner told me that I could stay with him until I found a place. After I worked my first shift as a stripper, I dreamed of better things in my future, understanding that this was just a stepping stone to reaching my goals.

Chapter 3
Marriage #1

There was a man in his 30s who came to the strip club where I worked. He would sit in front of me but not put money on the bar. Finally, I got mad at him because he would sit there watching and not pay any money. I looked at him and said, "Are you going to place some money on the table?"

"I don't give money to strippers," he said. "However, I will give you my number, and if you need anything, I will help you out."

I didn't know this man, but he looked like a man who had grown up in a good household. I thought I could trust him.

I had been staying with the owner of the strip club, and it started to get very uncomfortable at his house. He started flirting with me. "You know, you're going to have to pay me back somehow. Rent ain't free."

I looked at him and thought, *Dude, if I was making decent money at your bar, then I would not be here.*

One day, while I slept on the couch, the owner decided he was going to try to touch me. At that point, I knew it was time for me to leave. I had that man's number from the strip club. When I called him and told him what happened, he came to pick me up.

The first night that I stayed with him, I realized what an asshole this man truly was toward women. He seemed to view women as his property and had the misguided notion that he was like a God to women. He would constantly boast about all the women who liked him and wanted to be with him. I couldn't stand him at all. He informed me there was another strip club down the street where I could work and make good money since it was close to a military base.

Please know that I was stripping to get money for my apartment. I was in survival mode. I had no intention of making it a career.

However, it was easy money. There were times where I felt degraded as a woman, but I always had cash on hand. The man who helped me get out of that situation, the asshole that I couldn't stand, ended up sticking to me like a piece of gum on the bottom of my shoe. We started to date. I have no idea why I thought it was a good idea to be with this man. Probably because he promised me the world, and I was only 18 years old. I believed that he would do right by me. I had no idea what was to come in this new relationship.

Many times, I thought of my high school love. Was he okay? I wondered how badly I had hurt him, because I hadn't told him anything. The only thing I told him was that I was breaking up with him and that he deserved better than me. I had to start my adult life and he was still in school — there was no way that life was going to work out. Plus, he was underage, and his parents didn't like me. I later learned that I had sent him into a deep depression and all his dreams of being a Navy Seal were destroyed. He ended up becoming an alcoholic and at the age of 17, broke into a country store and stole alcohol. I still feel really bad about what happened to him, and I blame myself for him not achieving his goals.

Since I had started working at a different strip club, I was able to get my first apartment. I remember the feeling of being able to get my first place, somewhere that I could call home. I jumped up and down with emotions of achievement. I had no furniture, no plates, no television, but it didn't bother me. I knew eventually I would get all the things I needed to fill the space.

Being an adult is hard. I'd had no idea the amount of

responsibilities an adult had to shoulder. I would often reflect on the things that I hadn't had to worry about while I was a child. I also would reflect on what would have happened if I had just done what my parents told me to do. What kind of life would I have right now if only I had listened to them? Or what kind of career path would I have chosen if my parents had offered to pay for my college? I figured eventually I would go to college and get my degree, but it couldn't happen yet.

However, because of my impulsive decisions, I was in a situation where I had to grow up quickly and become an adult. For the most part, I enjoyed not having to answer to anyone. I didn't have any rules. I could wear the clothes I wanted to wear, and I could do what I wanted. It was kind of refreshing to be able to wake up in my own apartment, figuring out the list of things that I had to do before I started my shift. "Maybe being an adult isn't as hard as people are saying," I thought.

But I was not alone. The man who helped me get out of the house of the strip club owner was now my live-in boyfriend. This was another turning point in my life.

There is an expression that people sometimes repeat, "you will never find a husband in a bar." The meaning of this expression had never been explained to me. Men will, of course, try to take strippers home in order to have sex with them. However, I was not interested in any of these guys who handed me their number. I was already in a relationship with my boyfriend at this point. He would come to the strip club while I worked, almost as though he was my bodyguard.

I recall a time I was leaving the strip club and a man came behind me and grabbed my butt as I was walking out the door. I spun around and faced him. "I know you didn't just grab my ass," I said. When my boyfriend heard what I said, he punched this guy right in the face. I was glad that night he was there to handle that situation. "Maybe he really does love me if he is willing to protect me from other men," I thought. I had no idea at that moment he would not only be my first husband but also father to my oldest son.

My first marriage was very difficult for me. My first husband was an alcoholic who was very demeaning to women. He was mentally abusive to me and every woman in his family. We had only been together for about six months when I became pregnant with my first child.

Oh my God! Eighteen and pregnant! Since I was pregnant, I immediately stopped dancing. My boyfriend was doing side jobs, making money under the table. That was how we survived. I had a feeling God was telling me to make this relationship right by getting married. So, we decided to get married. The truth, however, was that I was not at all happy to be married to this man. His callous manner, combined with the lack of respect he showed to his parents and grandparents, broke my heart. Many people in his family couldn't believe that I was going to marry him in the first place.

I was not really in touch with my family at that time. Right before we were going to marry, I contacted my family and told them what was going on in my life. I do think that my mom was happy to hear that I was still alive at least.

Around that time, I had picked up a newspaper only to read that my dad's mom had passed away. This was the grandmother that I spent many hours with as a child. Whenever I got in trouble, I went to my grandmother's house and worked in her backyard or cleaned her house. I would also go over there when I wasn't in trouble as well.

I asked her once, "Grandma, do you go to church?"

She replied, "No, I don't need to go to church, because I have my church every day, all day long." She woke up every morning, drank her coffee, read the newspaper, and talked to Jesus. I asked her if she craved fellowship with her neighbors. She simply replied, "When I go and do my errands, I have fellowship. I speak to people about Jesus." Because I had always felt the same way, her answer made sense to me. Both of my grandmothers were so amazing. To this day, I miss them dearly.

It bothered me that I had to find out about my

grandmother's death by reading it in the newspaper. With that being said, I had not been in contact with my parents for them to tell me about her death or even the fact that she was very ill.

The funeral was scheduled for the same day as my wedding. I contacted my mom to invite her and my dad to the wedding; however, because of the funeral it was a schedule conflict for them, and they were not able to attend. Of course, this gave rise to feelings of being excluded from the family. Maybe, I thought, they just didn't want to have anything to do with me or the family that I was creating. Later, I realized that I completely had the wrong idea and was being very selfish.

The day before the wedding, my future husband had plans to go out with the boys for his bachelor party. When I went upstairs to put some clothes away, I saw him snorting cocaine. This was the first time I had ever been exposed to cocaine. I had smoked marijuana at the age of 17, but in my opinion it was peaceful. I was so mad at him for bringing that into my house. I couldn't believe that was in my house or that he was doing it in the first place. We argued and fought over the fact that he was doing it. He told me that he was sorry and would never do it again.

After the argument, he left with the boys for his bachelor party. Still, to this day, I have no idea what he did that night or where he went. I sat up all night worrying about what he was doing, and as a pregnant woman, all kinds of thoughts went through my head. I didn't get a bachelorette party. I was at home by myself watching television while I mentally prepared for this marriage. He eventually came home and passed out. I knew what he was doing was not right and putting our child in that kind of environment was not going to work. That was the first sign I received that this marriage might not succeed.

My first wedding day was one of the worst days ever. Of course, my husband was hungover for the wedding. I ended up setting it up by myself, getting the cake, and doing the decorating. We had planned on getting married in the backyard of our townhouse. I had hired a justice of the peace to perform the marriage; however, it was very weird and impersonal. It felt wrong. The entire time I was saying to myself, *This isn't what I wanted my wedding to be like.*

I wanted the traditional experience of a classy wedding. The planning of the wedding, the excitement of picking out the perfect dress, the venue, and, of course, the wedding rings. His mother and sister were at the wedding. But on our wedding night, he left me at home and went to a bar. We didn't even consummate our wedding vows. My life as a pregnant wife at home alone while my husband bounced from bar to bar had begun.

I was so happy to be pregnant. Finally, there was going to be one person in my life who would love me unconditionally: my child. The moment I found out I was pregnant, my whole outlook on life changed. It was a magical moment for me. "I am going to be a mom," I said to myself. "And I'm going to do it differently." I told myself all the things I would do for my child that I didn't get from all my parents in my life. I knew that I was always going to be there for my children, even during hard times. I was going to teach them unconditional love and respect for people around them. I hope that everyone gets to experience this feeling in life.

It was very hard being pregnant while my husband was out at a bar all the time. It caused a lot of fights between us. He felt as though he had every right to be out at the bars. I would try to explain to him that all I wanted was to be able to spend time with him. I was so lonely while I was pregnant. I did, however, talk to God a lot during this time. I started going to the church my then-husband's mother attended. It was a Baptist church that was right around the corner. I felt that maybe, just maybe, I could get my husband to start coming to church with me, and that would lead to it becoming a Sunday tradition for us.

There were signs that the marriage wasn't going to last. First, I could feel it in my soul. Beyond that, he did things like staying out until four o'clock in the morning. I honestly always thought he was cheating on me.

One night, when he stayed at the bar until four o'clock in the morning, I experienced a panic attack for the first time. I had walked out of the house to go to my sister-in-law so she could help me. On the way, I blacked out and fell to the ground. My sister-in-law was already on the way to pick me up when she found me on the ground. She called an ambulance to come and take me to the hospital to make sure that my son was okay.

This man had the nerve to look me in my face and say, "The only reason you are having a panic attack is because you wanted me to leave the bar."

I simply replied, "If you were not so much of an asshole and were here for your pregnant wife, then I wouldn't have panic attacks." Again, the lack of respect for women. He wasn't concerned that I had a panic attack or that I had fallen or even whether the baby was okay.

As a new mom, I tried to enjoy being pregnant even though my husband was not making it easy. There were some women who I turned to while pregnant to talk about the different stages during the pregnancy. I felt that I had clear signs that our baby was going to be a boy. One night, I had a dream that told me I was going to have a boy. The dream started with me going to an underground mall. In the mall, there was an acupuncture specialist. I walked in and she said to me, "Do you know the gender of the baby?"

"We have about four weeks before we find out if the baby is a boy or a girl," I explained to the dream woman.

"I can tell you the sex of the baby by doing acupuncture," she said.

In the dream, I was excited. I wanted to know, even though I already knew in my heart it was going to be a boy. I laid on her table to begin the acupuncture. I felt as though I had fallen asleep because boy images appeared to be floating in the air. I saw a cupcake with blue frosting on it with writing, "It's a Boy." I woke up the next morning in tears. Not sad tears, but tears of joy. I immediately started to talk to our son and call him by the name we had chosen.

The first time my son moved in my belly was amazing. I was so excited. I asked my husband to come share in the experience of feeling our baby move. "Come feel your son move," I said.

"No. It grosses me out," he answered.

What? All the questions started spinning through my head again. "Why does it gross you out? This is your blood, your son, you made this child. Why in the world would you not want to experience this moment with me?" I was so hurt by that comment. Never in my life did I think it would be said to me by my husband or the father of my child. Of course, this was a lesson in life for me yet again. I understood then that it is important not to rush into marriage. Pregnancy is not a reason to get married. I would have been better off being a single mom. There is support out there for single moms.

In October 2003, my biological mother died. I received a phone call telling me what had happened. She was standing on the side of the road trying to fix her truck, when a person driving a Ford Ranger took his eyes off the road and hit her.

She died instantly.

My brother was with his dad in Idaho. As a child, I'd had premonitions which always came true. This premonition came true, and it scared me to my core. Two weeks before this accident, I'd had a dream that she was hit by a white Ford Ranger and died.

This was always very interesting to me that I dreamed something and then it happened. Sometimes I wondered if my dreams actually manifested an event. I didn't understand until later in life that these dreams were messages from my guardian spirit.

The lawyer handling the case informed me that the vehicle that hit my biological mother was, in fact, a white Ford Ranger. I had been in contact with the lawyer because I was concerned about my brother's well-being.

My biological family pursued that company that the driver worked for, because he was driving a company truck. My mother had been leaving to deliver the goods to a new destination. The man driving the Ford Ranger had taken his eyes off the road, killed my mother and severely injured another driver. The other driver was someone my mother had been helping to fix his trailer. When I spoke with the attorney, I told him that he needed to sue them for the negligence of that driver. I wanted any monies from the lawsuit to be put into a trust for my brother. I didn't want any of the money because it wouldn't bring my mother back. I needed to make sure that because of this man being irresponsible, my brother would not want for anything in his life.

Since then, I have always listened to my dreams. We are all intuitive in our own ways. In life, we are supposed to master this skill and use it to help people.

There were so many things wrong about the death of my biological mother. I was concerned about my brother, where he was going to live, if this guy who I didn't like was going to raise my brother right, and what I needed to do to help him. Also, not to mention all the unanswered questions that I had not had the chance to ask my biological mother about my childhood. Who was my biological father? Why did she give me up? What should I do for my brother? Why would God take her when she had a nine-month-old at the house? I couldn't understand why God would take a loved one to heaven at such a young age. Then I came to the realization that the one thing that I longed for, the thing I'd wanted my entire life, which was to have a relationship with her, was not going to happen. Ever. That hope disappeared on the day we lost her.

I was pregnant, grieving, and needed support. My husband did not, or could not, give me anything to help me through this ordeal.

As I continued with life after losing my mother, I would often talk to her in the hope of having a paranormal experience while I was awake. At times, I sat in my living room thinking that I heard something or someone moving around even though I was alone in the house.

I think many people long to have a spiritual moment of connection with someone who has passed; it is in our soul. We tell ourselves, "I wish I could see them one more time, hold them one more time." However, they are holding us, trying to pass their energy to us every minute of every day. They whisper in our ear, "Just call my name."

Bringing a child into this world is the most magical experience that we can have in life. When my son was born, I didn't care about anything except him. I didn't even care if my husband was there or at the bar. I knew that my son was going to be my pride and joy over any man in my life. The one thing that I always wanted was to have children. I wanted to have the experience of creating life. I wanted to be the mom I thought every child should have. It often makes me wonder if God had the same feelings when creating this world.

The morning I was in labor, husband #1 took me to the hospital. Husband #1 had been out drinking the night before, so me going into labor was not the best time for him. On the way to the hospital, I told myself that I was not going to leave that hospital without my child in my arms. I figured that maybe if our son came, husband #1 would stay out of the bars. I hoped he would be the father and the husband he was supposed to be after he saw his child for the first time.

I didn't enjoy the pain of labor at all, but what woman does? Thank goodness the doctor and nurses were Johnny-on-the-spot with the pain medicine. It was funny; during labor, I was in so much pain that the nurse gave me a little too much pain medicine. I remember looking at my husband and saying, "Little purple Bart Simpson is taking my medicine out of the wall." The next time the nurse came in my room, I told her the same thing. She replied, "Let's turn this down just a little bit." I still laugh when I tell that story. It is always good to be able to laugh at yourself, it lightens the heart. Even though I was happy the pregnancy was over, and I was able to have my body back to myself, there was still a sense of dread about my marriage.

When my son was born, I thought (and still believe) he was the most beautiful person I had ever seen. I made sure that he had all 10 fingers and 10 toes. He weighed eight pounds, one ounce, and was 21½ inches long with white hair. My son was so beautiful it took my breath away. Of course, being a new mom, I was scared that I was going to drop him, maybe put his diaper on wrong, or do something incorrect during the process of being a mom. Women really don't give themselves enough credit for doing mom things. I didn't read any pregnancy books, I didn't go to any Lamaze class, and I didn't know what to expect during labor. I just did what the nurses and doctors told me to do, because giving birth is natural for women. Everything worked out just fine.

As I mentioned, my relationship with husband #1 was rocky from the beginning. We should have never gotten married. I considered leaving him after my son was born, however my spirit spoke and said, "Stick it out for our son." I think the main reason I wanted to persevere was because I knew what it was like to be from a broken family. I didn't want my son to have the same feelings as a child. Of course, I fell into the trap of thinking that once my son was born, our relationship would get better. Unfortunately, I was very naïve. In fact, our relationship only got worse.

We started off living the American dream: moving into a house with a swing set and a fenced-in backyard that would be a good place to raise a child. I wasn't working at the time, so I was able to have quality time with my son. During the day, we went on walks in a nearby park, we played in the backyard, and then it was nap time. We only owned one vehicle, and my husband worked as a home improvement man. It was very lonely at the house. However, I was grateful that I was able to have that time with my son.

My depression got bad after I had my son. Postpartum depression (what used to be called baby blues) is a real thing for women, and for women who are already depressed, it is 10 times worse. I wanted to die. I was desperately lonely, and my husband wouldn't talk to me about how I felt or what he could do to help me. The baby blues and my depression took a serious toll on me daily. This burden was in addition to a marriage which was completely going down the toilet.

My husband was a mean drunk all the time. He was out at bars almost every night. Because he was out at bars all the time, we hardly had any food in the house for us or our son. I'd had enough of his shit and decided I was done with this life. He had plenty of family around to help him raise our son. I wanted to leave this world. I was going to commit suicide. The refrain, *my son will be better off without me*, continually ran through my head. I was also convinced that I was unable to provide the things that my child needed in his life.

Depression ate away at my body and soul.

One day, everything changed. My husband had left some marijuana out on the counter. I contacted my sister-in-law to come pick up my son to spend the night with her so that I could have alone time. I had not slept in almost two days. The pain of depression was so unbearable, and all I wanted to do was sleep. After they left, I smoked some marijuana so I could calm my mind and go to sleep. All my depressed feelings went away when I smoked. I was at peace with myself. My mind was uncluttered of all the negative thoughts that I had been feeling for so long. I was able to think clearly, and my panic attacks stopped.

On a side note, marijuana is a natural plant substance. I am not condoning the use of hard drugs or the abuse of substances. For some women, a beer or glass of wine helps them have clarity in their lives. Marijuana affects people differently and some don't like the way it makes them feel. I didn't like how I felt when I drank alcohol, which is why I chose to use marijuana. I personally feel like there should be more research into this healing plant substance, so we can better understand its medicinal properties.

To all the moms in the world: we must remember to give back to ourselves. Mothers need down time so that they can recharge their energy for the next day. We give so much to the world but never enough to ourselves.

Then my world once again was turned upside down. It was husband #1's birthday. I was making a birthday meal for him so we could celebrate. I had worked all day to make this meal for him. He had been drinking the entire day. Right before it was time to put the meal on the table, he informed me that he was waiting for his ride. His plan was to go out with his friends all night, leaving me and our son at the house — alone — once again. At that point, I realized this man didn't want to be seen in public with me. His actions implied he was ashamed of us.

At that point, I was done with this marriage. This was not a marriage. I was a servant, not his wife or the mother of his child. I always thought it was weird that he habitually went to the bar without me, and I was never invited to go with him. Of course, I lost my mind. I was so done.

When his ride showed up, the driver was a woman. *Oh, okay*, I said to myself. *He is cheating on me, right to my face.* We hadn't had relations in at least a month, and when I saw her, I just knew. I couldn't understand why he was cheating on me. I had been faithful to him. *How long has this mistress been in the picture*, I wondered. *When did you give up on our marriage? Why would you do this to our family?* My entire marriage was in question.

I needed answers, so I called him on his cell phone and asked, "Who are you with, and why are you with her?"

His answer jolted me. "We are going to a hotel to fuck, and we are going to tape it for you." Then he hung up on me. Fire raced through my body, making me feel like a mad woman. With the anger came questions. I planned to confront him with my questions when he got home.

I would never receive answers. He was so drunk when he came home, he could barely stand up. I had to tell him that our son was sleeping and to be quiet. He called me a bitch, cunt, idiot, and said that he hated me. I was tired of him speaking to me in that way and so mad that I ended up spitting in his face. The next moment happened fast. I did not expect him to become physical.

He grabbed me by my throat and pushed me up against the door, choking me. He then turned and wrapped his arm around my neck, putting me in a choke hold. I thought he was going to kill me. I thought he was going to break my neck. My life flashed before me. Thoughts of my past, the life my son would live if I wasn't around. I was scared for my child — but not at all worried about me. I didn't want him to hurt my son. Eventually, I blacked out and woke up on the kitchen floor. When I realized what had happened, I grabbed the phone, ran to my son's room and locked the door.

He was still asleep in his crib, arms thrown over his head as his steady breath made his chest rise and fall. Thank God my husband had not messed with him. As I started to dial 911, a sudden pounding sounded on the bedroom door. "Give me my son," he yelled.

"911, what is your emergency?"

"My husband is drunk. He just choked me…"

The line disconnected and I was left talking to dead air. He must have unplugged the receiver to my phone. Now I had no way to contact the police, and I worried that he would break down the door. I looked around, frantic to escape, and realized the window was my only hope. I grabbed some items to take with me, scooped up the baby, and planned to climb out the window. As I held my son, I listened carefully, intent on staying alive.

I knew by the way he spoke he had called his sister. "I put my hands on her, and she called the police. What do I do?" His sister must have told him to leave the house because the next thing I heard was the door slamming. I guess he went to his sister's. I couldn't believe that his sister would tell him to leave the house. She knew the things that I had been going through, so why would she have his back at a time like this? She was going to be the next person I called to come get me, but now that option was gone.

I waited five minutes before I made my move. I took my son into my bedroom and locked the door. In that room, the phone was not disconnected. Thank the Lord the police called back because I was able to answer the phone. By the time I looked out the window, I saw a police car flying into the front yard. The police entered the house and made sure it was safe for me to come out of the bedroom. This very fearful night taught me so much. I was never going to let another man put his hands on me ever again. I had made a very bad choice in a man on my part. I did what I had to do to protect myself and my son.

At this point, I had no choice but to call my parents, hoping that they would be a rock for me. Hoping that the damage I had done to them would not make them turn us away. I called my mom while the police were in the house. We filed a report for abuse, pictures were taken, and an emergency protective order was issued against husband #1. Again, my mom and dad were in my corner; they had our back. Every time I have ever needed them, they were there. My son and I went home to my parents, the parents who have kept me safe all my life.

We went through the long battle of divorce, child

support, and custody. Of course, he wanted joint custody of our son. However, the court did not grant joint custody when an assault is involved. Husband #1 went into court disrespecting the judge, and she threw the book at him. Husband #1's face was priceless to look at when he was sentenced. *Maybe next time you will think before you put your hands on a woman*, I thought. She ordered him to pay $560 a month in child support and allowed him to have supervised visitation every other weekend. I would not see hardly any of the money. Seventeen years later, the debt is high. He is $56,000 behind in child support. I got tired of wasting money fighting for it and started using the lawyer's fees for my son. I always felt so bad that my son was going to experience the broken family dynamic. However, it was my job as his mother to provide protection and a stable living environment. I did what was best for him and myself at the time.

Despite claiming he wanted custody rights, my son's father was not there for him during his childhood. When it was his weekend, he would drop our son off at either his mother's house or his sister's house. My son would spend the night with his father's family watching movies but mostly it was his family spending time with our son. Husband #1 was out partying at the bar with his new girlfriend. I was grateful my son was able to have time with his grandparents and have that relationship.

I found over the years that husband #1's family was very confrontational when I dropped my son off. This was probably some of my fault as well because I had so much anger toward husband #1. Within less than a year, husband #1 had found another woman and she became pregnant. Husband #1 had already had a child prior to our relationship, however, the mother of his son would not allow any contact between father and son. So now he was going to be a father of three children that he didn't, or couldn't, see on a regular basis.

As my son and I began settling into a daily routine, we were able to enjoy life with much less drama. I started teaching my son how to play baseball when he was two years old. I loved playing baseball with him. He was so good, too. I thought that maybe it was hereditary because his dad used to play. He had received a baseball scholarship to James Madison University as their pitcher, but he tore his rotator cuff in the middle of the game. I had dreams that one day my son would be able to have that same opportunity.

Once, when my son was two years old, I threw the ball to him, and he hit it over my head. That is when I said, "This is going to be your sport, buddy." He has played ever since. I love watching him play. My son's father only came to one game. My son would ask his dad, "Are you going to come to my game?"

His dad would reply, "Of course I will be there."

At the game, I would see my son looking for his dad and then looking back at me, questioning the whereabouts of his father. Those days were so hard for me and my son. As a mom, my heart ached, feeling his emotions of disappointment in his little voice. I couldn't explain why his father wouldn't come to see him play. It hurt my son that his own father wouldn't support him like a father should. Here was that feeling of abandonment happening to my son again. This was the one thing that I had tried to prevent from happening to my son. I felt as though I had failed once again.

With the help and support of my parents, I was able to get a job so I could make some money. I ended up doing electrical work as a helper for a local electrical company. Working in a male-dominated field was an interesting experience. I didn't feel weird about doing construction. I have always been a very handy person with working on things. I had to get a job, but I still had no high school diploma. As I kept my hands busy with manual work, I was mentally healing from the trauma of the last year and a half.

The divorce was very difficult to get through only because of the lack of cooperation from husband #1. Fortunately, I was blessed to have parents who helped me financially with the court costs and the custody battle. I was not going to feel comfortable leaving our son with him after he demonstrated his proclivity toward violence and put his hands on me. I didn't even trust him to have our son without supervision on his weekends. When we split up, the items that I had collected were left in the house. I was going to have to start all over again: new furniture, new clothes, all the household things that one needs to have a home. Most importantly, I had a new chance in life. Just another experience under my belt. I learned to take the lesson and let it go.

Since my son had been visiting his father every other weekend, I had extra time to focus on myself for a while. However, this ended when my son came home and told me that his father was never there with him. My son also told me that he was sleeping on the floor with the dogs. Upon more investigation, it was brought to my attention that husband #1 was involved with a woman who was selling cocaine. At that point, I was not going to have my son live in that kind of environment. There were times when my son and I were not getting along, and I recall him telling me, "Mom, I don't want to live with you anymore." Kids say things like that, but my heart was crushed. I couldn't believe he felt like that toward me. I cried for many hours that night, just trying to understand why. When I picked him up later from his father's house, my eight-year-old son looked at me and said, "Mom, I don't want to go back to my dad's."

I replied, "Okay, son, I will go to court and stop visitation." So back to court we went to fight for what my son wanted in his life. My son told the guardian ad litem that he didn't feel safe staying with his father. The court stopped visitation immediately. If I haven't achieved anything in my life, the one thing I made sure of was that I fought for my children. I was continuously stressed and worried during this process of trying to get our life together.

I had not truly healed from the divorce or the abusive relationship before I dived right into the next chapter in my life. On my way home from work while driving across the bridge, I saw a guy in a red Toyota pickup truck. For some reason, I thought he was kind of cute. At the time, I did not know that I was going to end up dating him for five years of my life with a child in tow.

Chapter Four
Marriage #2

At the age of 19, I had a child and a divorce under my belt. I met husband #2 when I was coming home from work. This man was different from my first husband. I thought, *Okay, I know I don't want a man who drinks a lot.* This man did not, and two or three drinks were his limit. I thought this was a good sign that he was not an alcoholic but I didn't consider anything else. The relationship moved fast again. It was almost like my first marriage. He lived on his mother's land, close to where my parents lived. This man was much older than my ex-husband. I figured that he was more mature and that this would be a completely different relationship.

Not long after meeting husband #2, I ended up getting into a fight with my parents because they were trying to give me advice which I didn't want to hear. They told me that I was rushing into this relationship and needed to slow down. My parents were concerned that this was not healthy for me or my child. I still didn't have my GED or a college degree. My parents told me that I needed to put my priorities in order. Of course, my reaction was outrage that they would try to tell me how to run my life. I was so mad at them for trying to control my life that I left. I was done. I didn't want to waste time and money on college when I had a job. These were my thoughts at the time.

Shortly after this fight, I moved in with husband #2 on his mother's land. Unfortunately, the house left much to be desired. He lived in a shack without running water or a bathroom. To this day, I have no idea why I did this to myself and my son, but I would like to think that the decision to live like this provided me with the desire to never live like that again. There I went again, making not such a good decision, but I went ahead and moved in to the shack with him. His mother lived in an apartment over the garage on the property. We used the shower in the garage. Living like this with a child never felt comfortable or right. Unfortunately, I didn't have any savings and couldn't get an apartment yet.

I continued working in the electrical field for a big commercial construction company. At this point in the relationship, I was unaware that husband #2 was doing pills or that he had an addiction. This didn't become clear until I had an accident at work. While I was pulling wire from a ceiling to a floor outlet, 15 pieces of a 12 x 6 pile of sheetrock fell on my shin and broke it at a 90-degree angle. This situation really put childbirth into perspective for me. Labor was a piece of cake compared to this. The pain was unbearable. It took eight men to lift the pile off my leg. As soon as they were able to get the pile of sheetrock off me, I fell to the floor in agony. The guy I was working with at the time tried to be helpful. He stood next to me and said, "Girl, you got this. I have been stabbed, I have been shot, you got this."

I looked him in the eye and said, "If you don't shut the fuck up, I will beat you with this broken leg." I was in so much pain I didn't give a rat's ass about him being stabbed or shot, I just wanted something to make the throbbing stop in my leg.

The paramedics rushed to my side. They told me that they were going to give me some medicine through an IV in my arm. I was also told that they were going to roll me on the carry board and pop my leg back in place. Thank the Lord it was a quick roll and a lot of pain medicine. I began to go into shock for a minute. They rushed me to the nearest hospital so the doctor could examine my leg. I had a clean break in my shin, affecting my tibia and fibula. The doctor ordered me out of work for six months.

They then put me in a full leg cast and sent me home with Oxycodone.

This was the first time I had ever broken a bone in my life. The doctors loaded me up with the strongest pain pills possible. It was a very long road to recovery. Needless to say, I had no idea that the medicine my doctor prescribed was going to lead me to become an addict.

Unfortunately, husband #2 started stealing my pain pills. This was a big problem for me when I went to take my medicine and all of it was gone. I was in pain, and there was nothing I could do to ease the pain. I confronted him about this, and he said, "I won't do it again."

I had to return to the doctor who was treating me to get more medicine for the pain. The medical professionals told me that at this point in the healing process, I should not be having so much pain. However, the doctors would prescribe more medicine for me so that I could sleep. I couldn't stand the recovery process — it was taking too long to heal my leg. It seemed that the doctor was very old and not well informed about updated medical processes. The doctor couldn't get my bones to line up correctly. I asked if there was any way that we could speed the healing process up. The doctor suggested surgery to put a metal rod in my tibia. The pain was unbearable, and I ended up having to take many pills during the day just to manage the pain as I was trying to take care of my son. Of course, the result of this was an addiction to pain pills. This addiction took hold of me quickly. I loved not feeling any pain, and honestly, if the doctor was prescribing it, then there was nothing wrong with me taking it, right?

Until now, I never reflected on the fact that I had a child to take care of and the importance of being a sober parent for him. My only option, it seemed, was to remain focused on not being in pain while still being able to function as a mom. He was so young at the time that he didn't know what I was doing. While taking the pills, I could still function and work, performing daily tasks. I wasn't in pain while I was on the pain pills. I was numb again. However, it became more difficult to obtain the pills, because the doctor eventually refused to prescribe them to me. This behavior of taking pills and moving from doctor to doctor for more prescriptions continued for many years. Then we started buying them.

After my injury, I received worker's compensation because it had been a job-related accident. We ended up getting a cheap apartment in the downtown area. It was a one bedroom with a kitchen and living room. At that point, we had been dating for four years. During the time that we lived at that apartment, we witnessed many troubling incidents. Our apartment was on the second floor. The neighborhood that we were living in was not a very safe area to raise a child. However, it was what we could afford at the time. Our building had an entrance door that was locked except for the people in the building who had a key. Once, a man decided he would commit suicide by jumping off the balcony of his apartment. There was one morning I opened my front door to get my newspaper and blood was smeared all over the walls. The man who lived on the third floor had been stabbed the previous night in our hallway. It wasn't long before I was ready to leave that apartment. I never thought that I would have to wake up to an image of blood in my apartment building. This was not a place to raise a child. This was not how we were supposed to live.

Right before I met husband #2, his father had died from an overdose of pills. When I look back on the situation, he had been doing more drugs than I had during the course of our relationship. When I started asking him questions about his addiction, he explained that his addiction started at a very young age. Husband #2 also told me that he was on pills when we first met. He had been taking methadone and pills while still functioning for work. At this point, I had lived with him for so many years and heard so many apologies that I thought this was the relationship I was supposed to be in. I assumed my life was bound to have conflict, drama, betrayal, addiction, and misery. So, I stayed where I was, doing the same shit every day and not wanting to try to change my situation for my son. I thought I was in love with this man. I really didn't have respect for him, and honestly, I don't think he respected me, because he would still cuss at me and call me bitch, cunt, asshole, and all kinds of names. I thought this was how love worked. Couples fight. They call each other names, then they fight about the problem, and all is well again. That is not a healthy relationship. Arguing does not give you the right to talk down to your partner.

At some point, we learned that husband #2 was set to receive an inheritance from his father's estate. This was great news for him. He could now get a truck to replace the one he had wrecked while being high. Plus, he wanted to move to the county where there was a lot of land. So, we started searching for a home about an hour away from my parents. Meanwhile, we became pregnant with my second son. It really wasn't a surprise, but it was going to change my life once again. The weird part is that I remember the night that my second son was conceived. I knew there was something very special about this child, as if we were connected spiritually.

During my pregnancy, I did not take drugs. I completely stopped, but my husband continued to indulge. I also thought that things were going to be different in our relationship, because we were going to be able to get a house where we could raise the boys.

Husband #2 was very happy that he was going to be a dad. He did all the things that new dads are supposed to do when they learn about their baby. He touched my stomach when our baby moved. He laid in bed with his head on my stomach, talking to his son. Once, he was talking to the baby, and my son kicked him right in the face. We were not married when our child was conceived because I had already been through a divorce and didn't really want to marry him at that moment, even though we had been together for five years. The voice of spirit was telling me that this relationship was not going to last.

The entire family was thrilled to have another child added to our blended family. My oldest son was excited; he wanted a brother. While pregnant with my second child, I didn't receive any gender reveal information in my dreams. I did, however, have a feeling that it was going to be another boy. Honestly, when we found out that it was a boy, I thanked God for the blessing. I felt that I would not be able to raise a girl. Before I discovered that my children were going to be boys, I had prayed to God to give me boys, simply knowing what my parents had gone through with me. I felt as though I couldn't handle dealing with a little girl.

At this time, I kept my parents informed of what was going on in my life. They had a relationship with my oldest son, who often spent the night with his grandparents. This kept the lines of communication open between my parents and me. I figured that since my mother hadn't been in the delivery room for my first son, I would ask her to be in the delivery room for the birth of my second son.

Unfortunately, my labor experience the second time was way more painful than the first time. My pain medicine wasn't working because I had become immune from all the pain medicine that I had been taking for so many years. The doctors refused to give me stronger pain medicine. The doctor did give me an epidural; however, it only worked on one side of my body. I was thankful the delivery was quick this time. I went into the hospital at 8:00 a.m., and my son was born by 5:09 p.m. He weighed seven pounds and 15 ounces and was $20^{1}/_{2}$ inches long.

I had the same feeling with my second child that I had with my first child. My second son was just as beautiful as his brother had been when he was born. I felt so blessed that I had my children, who I loved with all my heart and soul. I was amazed by what I had created to share with this world. I felt that I was the luckiest mother in the world to have two healthy children who were so beautiful. As I sat in the hospital looking at the family I had helped to create, I wondered if I was supposed to marry the father of my second son. I was scared but felt that it might be a good idea to make the family complete.

I was only 22 years old when I had my second son. While I was still in the hospital after the delivery of my second child, I reflected on my life and concluded that I had plenty of children. I worried that I was going to have a hard time providing them with what they needed since I wasn't getting any child support for my oldest child. At that moment, I made the decision to have my tubes tied while I was still at the hospital. I informed the doctor that I wanted her to tie my tubes. Not just tie them but cut and burn the tubes. The doctor informed me that they normally didn't do that procedure for women under 25 years of age. I felt very strongly about this and insisted the doctor perform the procedure. She went ahead and did the procedure before I left the hospital with my child. In the years since I've made this decision, I have regrets. I wish every day that I had listened to my doctor at the time.

Husband #2 received his inheritance from his father's estate. Shortly after the birth of our son, we decided that we had been together for almost five years, and now that we had a child, we should probably get married. Obviously, I hadn't learned my lesson from the first marriage, because here I went getting married not for love, but for the fact that I had a child with this man. I knew that this marriage was not going to work out either; it was just going to be another wound on my heart.

After having a sober conversation (on my part) with husband #2, I honestly thought things were going to change. I told him I was sober now, and he needed to be too, for himself, for me, and for the children. They deserved a family who could provide them with a great life. He had recently received his inheritance and swore to me that he was going to create that dream life with me. He was going to become sober like I was. Yet, I ignored my gut feeling and decided to go through with the marriage. About a month after my second son was born, we went to Kissimmee, Florida and tied the knot with a justice of the peace at the courthouse.

We started to argue more after our son was born. Because we had been together for a long time, I figured this was how the relationship was going to be. People had told me that fighting is inevitable in a marriage, but you need to forgive the conflict and move on. I didn't want a relationship where we fought every day. I wanted a husband who respected me, loved me, didn't talk down to me, and provided the emotional support in the relationship that would make it last forever. We were back to taking drugs, and oddly, that was when it felt like the relationship was going smoothly.

Sadly, I was very mistaken about what this marriage could give me.

Despite my unhappiness in the relationship with all

the drugs, one aspect of my life shifted at that point. We were able to get a house in the country. It was a rent-to-own mobile home with about two acres. The house sat in front of a man's property that had horses which the kids loved to go see every day. It was nice to live in the country, it was so peaceful. Though the area that we moved to was very isolated, I felt it was a good place to raise the children. But there were some downsides to living in the country, too. It was inconvenient to drive an hour to go to the grocery store, and I was not able to work because we could not afford childcare for two children.

Husband #2 had a job with a local electrical company until he hurt his back and could not work. The doctor ordered and scheduled surgery for his back, which allowed him to continue to take pills. About six months after receiving his inheritance, which totaled $123,000, the money was gone. The strength of his addiction had grown so much, the pills weren't working for him anymore. So, he started using hard-core drugs that were easily accessible in the area where we lived.

When he brought these drugs into our family dynamic, I was upset. "This is not what we should be doing," I said.

"It's okay," he said. "The kids are too young to notice anything."

My depression came back much worse after I had my second son. I was just so miserable with my life. When I looked in the mirror, I saw failure. I was such a failure to my parents, my child, my God, and myself. So, to escape the pain of being a failure, I start taking pills again to numb the internal pain in my heart.

We ended up buying heroin, cocaine, marijuana, and methadone. The addiction to the drugs got so bad. I carried a constant feeling that I was never going to amount to anything in my life. The revolving habit of numbness I got from taking drugs was the only thing that helped me get through the day.

Once, I left husband #2 to watch the kids while I went to the grocery store. Upon my return, I found him passed out on the couch with our youngest child face down on the floor, screaming. At that moment, I knew that I was not able to trust him with my children anymore. Husband #2 stated that our son was fine, and he wasn't hurt. He accused me of overreacting to the situation, a typical response from him. Whenever we had a fight, he always said I was overreacting. I finally looked at him and said, "You aren't reacting enough."

But I stayed because I felt like I didn't deserve any other way of life. The drug addiction had clouded my thinking, leaving me with the thought that no one would love me like he claimed to love me. I didn't even love myself. In fact, I hated myself so much for all the things I had done in my life. I hated the way I was living, not thinking of the consequences that would follow for myself and my children if anyone found out. My drug addiction was a secret. I still functioned, and no one ever realized that an hour before I had been in the bathroom snorting heroin up my nose in order to escape my negative thoughts.

My life was not what I imagined it should be, and that was a painful reality. I was trying to escape the sting of failure, so I started snorting the drugs that husband #2 had in the house while still maintaining my responsibilities as a mother and a wife. I didn't think that there was anything wrong with what I was doing as recreational use. While I was high, the feeling of pain left my heart. For a brief period, I snorted heroin, but it made me deathly ill. I stopped doing heroin and just continued taking Xanax, cocaine, and marijuana.

I knew it was wrong. It felt wrong. I had made a big deal about husband #1 doing it and having it in the house. I was such a hypocrite for doing the things that husband #1 was doing to cause him to have supervised visitation. I would often ask myself what made me any different from husband #1. Nothing. Absolutely nothing. We had blown through all that money and had nothing to show for it.

I was trying to get a job, however. I had been out of work for about two years. It got to the point where we were about to lose the house. Husband #2 was not able to work due to the back surgery that he'd had several months prior. We needed money quickly, so I went back to stripping. When I told him that I was going to go strip, he said to me, "Go make me proud." At that moment, I lost all respect for him as a man, husband, and a father. To be able to look at your wife, who is having to put herself in danger of being raped or sexually abused in order to put food on the table and be so cavalier about it, was nauseating. I was pissed that he was even encouraging me to do this.

There were times when I came home and caught him on the computer watching porn with what looked like underage girls. This really hurt me. I couldn't understand why he watched porn when I was willing to have sex with him, if that was what he wanted. Here I was going out and stripping to have a way to hold on to our house and put food on the table, while he sat at home watching porn. I don't know what I expected when I chose to stay with him. I felt ashamed of the decisions I had made over the course of our relationship and my life.

I met a girl who lived across the street from my house. We started to hang out all the time. She introduced me to crack cocaine. I was so disappointed with how my husband was acting and all the fighting that I just gave up on myself. She also told me I could make lots of money doing private parties. I had never done private parties before. The first night that I did a private party, I made $350. I was completely shocked at how much money I brought home that night. Honestly, the only way I was able to do private parties was to do so many of these drugs. My drug addiction got so bad that it started to really change my demeanor. I was angry all the time, yelling at husband #2 and my children for stupid things.

Finally, something had to change. I'd had enough of that lifestyle.

I met a lady through a church group close to where I lived. She shared with me her past of drug addiction and how she turned to God to get relief from the addiction. When she shared this with me, it felt as if this person had been chosen to speak to me to guide me back to God. She said, "Even though you have sinned in your life, if you repent and change your ways, God will forgive you. You are God's child, and he loves you unconditionally, like your parents do." Hearing these words was the first step back into the light while having hope and faith that God was going to help with this addiction — or so I hoped.

We were low on money, and I was so stressed about us getting ready to lose the house that I just thought if I could get a cocaine fix, I would be able to get through one more night of stripping for nasty old men. I went to my dealer and asked him to give it to me without paying. I assured him that I would pay him back once I got paid.

He agreed, but two weeks later, the drug dealer wanted his money. This was the reality check that did it for me. The drug dealer showed up in my front yard, with my children running around, acting as if he had a gun in his pants and might use it on me or my children. In a split second, my life and my children's lives flashed before me. This was not how I was supposed to live. My heart was racing, because husband #2 had no idea that I had asked for a front for drugs and this man was in his front yard acting like he was going to shoot someone. Husband #2 was either going to get shot or was going to die trying to protect me and the children. I told the drug dealer to leave, and I would go get his money. In that moment, I decided that I was not going to raise my children like this anymore. I was not going to put my children in harm's way again. My children deserved so much more in life, and I had to get myself together for them.

Husband #2 was pissed that I had not paid the drug dealer. He was mad that I put our son's life in danger because of drugs. Ironically, he was the one who introduced that behavior into our family, and he conveniently forgot that he was taking drugs too.

Things had to change, and I finally understood I had to take the right steps to reclaim my life. I started by telling husband #2 that I was done with our relationship. I was not in love with him anymore. There had been so much damage, lack of trust, lack of respect, and lack of security for the family that there was no way to fix the marriage. I was not going to live like this anymore. This conversation lasted all of ten minutes. I packed my clothes and some of the kids' belongings so we could start over. Once again, I called my parents. I told them that I had to move back home immediately, and I would explain what was going on when I got there. I packed only the necessary things my kids and I needed and returned to my parents. Husband #2 returned home to his mother's house.

Another divorce under my belt. Another lesson learned: don't get involved with someone who has a heavy drug addiction. I still smoked marijuana, which prevented me from going into withdrawal from all the drugs that I was getting out of my system.

There was a lot of stress that came with moving back home. I was so scared of what my parents were going to say or do because of all the dangerous behavior I had engaged in after leaving their house for so many years. My mom was very worried about my health, mentally and physically. I was very underweight. It looked like I hadn't eaten in months. To this day, I am so grateful that I had a place to go that was safe for my children.

My parents were not aware that I continued to smoke marijuana while living under their roof, but I felt it was necessary for me to maintain my sanity. As always, my parents were there to support me in getting back on track with my life. When I returned home, I got a job at 7-11 working nights. My parents told me that I needed to get my GED and go to college. My mom helped me with the process of getting my GED and then enrolling in college. I promised them this time that I was going to get my GED and a college degree. They told me they were going to be there to help me with the boys.

My second husband moved back to the shack on his mother's land. We went through the divorce process, which I paid for because he was still doing drugs. The court ended up awarding custody to me and every other weekend visitation for his father. Currently, husband #2 is still living in the shack on his mother's land. We had many custody hearings due to the fact that husband #2 was not caring for our son like he should have been. On more than one occasion, my son had been burned at his father's house. When that happened, his father didn't take the proper medical steps to care for the wound. Both of my sons had been hurt while in the care of husband #2 because he was still taking pills.

The scariest event occurred when my youngest was about two years old. He had gone to spend the night with husband #2 and his girlfriend at the time. The next morning, husband #2 was in the bedroom with his girlfriend at about lunch time while our son was on the front porch where a remodel was in progress. Electric tools were scattered everywhere on the front porch; it was not a childproof area. My son had picked up a torch and ignited it while pointing it at the top of his ear. He received a third-degree burn on his ear. When I asked husband #2 about it, I discovered my son had been left unsupervised, and he had not been taken to the doctor. At that point, I realized that I was the only responsible parent for my son.

I took him straight to his primary care doctor, and my two-year-old son told the doctor what happened to his ear. When I asked husband #2 what had happened, he stated once again I was overreacting. I was dumbfounded that my son's father would not take him to the doctor or even let me know that there had been an accident. I couldn't understand the lack of nurturing that was displayed in this situation. This was the point when I realized that he had never displayed responsibility like a parent should. His mindset was "boys will be boys." It sent me through the roof. The audacity of this man to say that statement provided much needed closure on our relationship.

On three separate occasions, my children received third-degree burns because they were not being watched carefully. The boys were very young when husband #2 was in their life. Both boys would still spend the night with husband #2. I would often ask husband #2 if he had planned on getting his own apartment to better his life, but the addiction was taking a huge toll on him. My boys loved spending time with husband #2 while he was in their life until they got hurt physically or emotionally. That was when they decided that they did not want to have that kind of drama in their lives.

I wanted the boys to have the relationship that every child should have with their father or father figure. It was important for them to learn things that only a male or father was supposed to teach them while they were young. When they were younger, it was a struggle to see them suffer from the lack of parenting that their dads were not providing. I was always the bad mom because I had rules and disciplined them when they got in trouble. There were so many times that my children would look at me and tell me that they wanted to go live with their fathers. This statement always put a wound on my heart, only because I was afraid that they would have to experience the same trauma as I did. However, I had to stand my ground as a mother, and I was not going to let their fathers continue to put them in harm's way.

But eventually everything changes. Both of my boys decided about the time they were eight years old that they didn't want to visit their fathers anymore. They had been hurt so much and were done with dealing with the drama, pain, and lack of affection that came with their fathers. I have kept my promise to protect my children and fight for what they want in life. Since the kids were minors, I hired an attorney to fight for full-time custody once again. As I juggled work, school, and the court system, I was able to provide a proper lifestyle for my children. I had one of the children enrolled in school, the other went to daycare. It was a stable environment, and the boys thrived.

Going back to court, though, meant I had to miss several days of work. This began to take a toll on me. Our court system is not the most efficient, and cases often drag out for longer than expected. Husband # 1 would call the court clerk to inform them that he was not going to be able to make it, and it needed to be rescheduled many times despite the fact that he had been subpoenaed to appear. Husband # 2 was not able to show up for court because he was high on pills and had lost his driver's license due to totaling his truck. It was a long battle, but the court finally ordered that until my son's fathers had a permanent residence that provided the standard living conditions, they would not see their fathers. To this day, my children do not have a relationship with their fathers.

During my short time of being back at home with my parents, I was able to get my GED while I worked at night. When I received my GED, I felt as though I had achieved so much in such a short period of time. The next step was to enroll in college. I was so excited to be able to get my life back on track for my kids. That was the first time in my life that I felt accomplished. That following semester, I started attending community college. It was hard for me to have patience because I wanted my degree in the shortest time possible. I completed one semester at the community college and then switched to a non-profit school to receive my degree.

I received an Associate Degree in Applied Science in Business with a concentration in Management. I decided that would be a good career for me to operate and manage my own business. I had a number of business ideas yet no knowledge of how to make it happen. I felt that pursuing a degree was a good decision to put me on the right path in my life. Once I had my GED, and I was enrolled in college, I felt a sense of relief and was able to enjoy being 24 years old.

My social life consisted of going to a local bar when I wasn't working. I slept all day, leaving my mother to take care of my children, then I would get up before I had to go to work to spend time with my kids. I would feed them dinner, give them a bath, and put them to bed, then off to work I went.

Chapter Five
Marriage #3

During this time while I was working at 7-11, there were so many men who asked me out. Since I had just left marriage #2, I was not interested in getting involved in a relationship any time soon. I just wanted to have fun. I had already been through two bad relationships, and I was not about to rush into another. The feelings that I had toward men were based on my past experiences. I believed that every man was a dog. Until one night when a handsome police officer came in my store. I wanted to talk to him so badly, but I was afraid to strike up a conversation. In three short months, my world changed for the better.

As a young woman working at 7-11, I was fortunate to meet some great people. I would have my regular customers who came in my store, but it was the policeman who came into the store at night I wanted to talk to. Every time he came in, I told the person that I worked with that I was going to be with that man. I wanted to know his story. I wanted to learn everything about him all in one day.

This police officer was very shy. He didn't talk much like the other customers who would sit there and talk my ear off almost my whole shift as if they didn't have anything else to do but be at 7-11. It was so very weird that when he would come in to get his cigarettes and beer, he would not look me in my face. I couldn't understand. It was almost like he didn't have any self-esteem. Like someone had told him he wasn't going to amount to anything in life. He had a nice car, a career, and a house, so there was no need for his self-esteem to be shattered. However, it is not just women who have wounds on their hearts, as I have found out. Men have wounds on their hearts from their mothers when they were in the womb.

This man came into my store every day for three months. He didn't say anything to me except for the items he wanted to pick up. Later, I found out that he had just recently ended a two-year relationship at the time that he was coming into my store. I felt as though he was out of my league and for me to even consider having a conversation with him was out of the question.

Finally, after some time passed, there was a night that I was working, and I was able to strike up a conversation with this man.

I took a deep breath and said, "Where are you coming from?"

He replied, "A concert. My friend plays in the band."

I had never heard of the band. That was when I started my small flirting tactics with him whenever I saw him in the store. I asked if he was married or had a girlfriend. Thirty minutes passed, and I had this feeling that he was not going to ask for my number. So, I asked for his. I was surprised that the words even came out of my mouth, and I thought that he would say, "No." However, he had a shocked look on his face which I assumed was his reaction to my question. A moment passed before he said, "Yes." I was completely taken aback. I couldn't believe that this handsome man, who had his shit together, would even talk to me.

For the next several days, we talked via text all day long. We learned small details about each other, including the things we liked and didn't like in a relationship. I told him that I had been divorced twice. That I also had two boys who were ages six and two.

It was amazing that he was still interested in me after everything I told him. I really didn't think that he would stay interested in me once he learned I had children. For most men, when a single mom announces that she has children, they run in the opposite direction.

Every morning, he sent a good morning text when he woke up. It reminded me of how new relationships began in high school. Back in school, the only option was to hand the person the note that you wrote the night before while they were entering their classroom. When we went to school, cell phones were not allowed. Every time I woke up and saw his text, I got butterflies in my stomach. This was how our relationship started; never did I think that I was going to get married again. In fact, I believe I said I would never marry again.

Our first date was amazing! I was so nervous that I was going out with a police officer only because of the things that I had done in my past that he was not aware of. I didn't know if he was going to judge me due to some of the things that had happened in my life. I worried he wouldn't want to date me because of my past drug use. I also wondered if being an upfront person would eventually scare him away. These were some of the thoughts racing through my head while getting ready for this exciting first date. I had a full conversation with myself in the mirror. I am so weird, I know.

He pulled up to my parent's house to pick me up for our first date. Oh, he looked amazing.

I was in complete awe.

He has green eyes and brown hair that are out of this world, and he even smelled good, too. Then he got out of the car and open the door for me. He drove a white and red 2008 Dodge charger. It was one of those hot rod cars. I felt like I was something special sitting in that car with him.

I was smitten. I had never had someone open the car door for me on a date. It was such a delight to have a traditional southern gentleman to go on a date with. Someone who was raised to respect women. It was not the case in my other two marriages. I have since taught my boys to treat women with respect and honor, for they are the givers of life. Also, always open the door for a woman even if she isn't your date.

As we drove to go on our date, my hands were shaking so much that I had to sit on them to keep him from seeing. I was very nervous. This was an amazing experience for me — having a genuine man taking me out. I could tell that his past relationships had caused him to put a wall around his heart. I had been through so much in my life, and I felt as though I was broken beyond repair. I believe he felt the same way about himself as well. He felt broken beyond repair and that he was not going to find someone to love him unconditionally. Most of the men that I had chosen to date were not the best of heart, and from what I could tell about this man, he was a good man. We rode into town to a local bar where a band was playing for the night. It was going to be a fun night of drinking, eating, and dancing.

While we were on our first date, we decided that we were not looking for anything serious, because we had both just gotten out of serious relationships that resulted in heartache. I wanted to make sure that he knew everything about me. Honestly, I had figured it was only going to be a one-time date with this man after he heard my life story. He had his life together. My thoughts were why would he want to start a relationship with someone like me. Here I was, a single mom of two who had been through one divorce already and was going through another. I didn't have a career, and I lived at home with my parents. So, I said to myself, "I am just going to tell him everything about me, and if he doesn't like me, okay, back to my life again."

We got to the bar, and because there weren't many people there, we were able to learn a lot about each other. I spilled my guts to him over a game of pool and several shots (maybe 15 or so) of vodka. I have never laughed so hard in my life. It felt so good to be able to laugh again. The band was a local rock band. We ended up rocking out like we were at a concert with a major band. He dropped me off at my house after an amazing first date. When he brought me home, I decided alright, he had a nice time. Maybe we would have one more date, but I was sure he wasn't going to take me to meet his family. As we stood at my parent's doorstep saying our good nights, we decided that we would like to go on another date soon. That was the night I was able to let all my wounds out to someone without the fear of judgement. I was able to speak my truth for the first time in life. A spark entered my heart. It was so easy to talk to him.

There have been several times in my life where I felt that I was not worthy of having a soul mate. I figured that since I had been so broken, I could never be loved by someone. It feels like this inner conflict has been in my life since birth. So, as I started dating this man, there was always this little voice that would whisper this relationship wouldn't last. As I went to bed that night, I thought of him and all the fun times we could have together.

I had no idea those dreams were going to come true.

In this relationship — if it became a relationship — I told myself that it was going to be completely different from the past. If there was a conflict, I was not going to let it sit on my mind and heart. I said to myself, "I will not go to bed angry. I did that in my last relationships, which didn't work."

As we started on this journey together, we agreed on several ground rules, and that was one of them. That was something that we both learned from past experiences.

It was important to me that we waited to introduce my children into the relationship. In my last marriage, I had jumped right in with my child, and it was an emotional rollercoaster for my boys. I had no intention of doing that to them again. I recognized that even though I was not happy, the kids still loved the male figure in their lives. They were still fathers to my kids, and I needed to show some compassion for my children. I knew that if I were to introduce the kids into the relationship and this man decided he didn't want to see me anymore, I was just putting them back on that emotional rollercoaster.

Another lesson learned. Protect your children emotionally.

This agreement allowed us to have time to build the foundation for our relationship. When we got together, we agreed that every relationship must have a foundation. We used the metaphor of a relationship as a house. The foundation is what holds the house up on solid ground. The foundation is trust. The walls were associated with communication. The roof was protection. I wasn't sure exactly where this relationship was going, but I was interested in testing the waters with this man. Our foundation was formed in the beginning and carries on to this day.

When we were dating, we had the best time. We talked all day and couldn't wait to see each other. I had butterflies in my stomach all the time. I had this feeling every time he texted me, every time he looked at me, and every time we touched. In all my relationships, I never felt so free to be me. I knew then that this man was my soul mate. I could say some of the stupidest shit, and he would burst out laughing at me. He made me feel as though he was going to be there for me always and forever.

We always laughed and messed with each other. Laughter is what bonds a relationship. One night, we went out on a date as we were still getting to know each other. Politics became the topic for a moment. I hadn't really been mindful about our government or politics. My thoughts are that our government has forgotten what this country is about and ignores the American people's needs and wants for their lives. I had voted one other time when I was 18 and at the time we were dating, I hadn't voted since.

During our conversation about politics, I told him, "I am going to Washington state to give the president a piece of my mind."

This beautiful man looked at me with a smile and a laugh and said, "That's not where the president lives."

I said, "Yes, it is. He lives in Washington, DC."

As he sat there laughing at me, he said, "Washington, DC, near Virginia." Still laughing at me, then he said,

"I'm going to the restroom, and I would like for you to think about that for a moment."

So, I sat there, thinking. Now mind you, I'd had five pineapple upside-down martinis when I decided to make my statement about going to talk to the president. I said to myself, "Oh, the president is only three hours away from me right now. We could make a weekend trip of going to see the president."

He came back to the table laughing, because he saw the look on my face of, "I just had a blonde moment." To this day, he still laughs at me about that. The story is always used as an ice breaker when we go to parties.

Another one of my blonde moments happened when we were going to meet his mother at a local pub. I drove a bright yellow Ford mustang. I loved that car. I felt like I was driving Bumblebee from the movie "Transformers." I had been running late to meet him and his mother, so I drove a little too fast. As I pulled into the parking lot, I hit the brakes too late and barely tapped the wall in front of my parking space. He got out of his mother's vehicle, laughing his head off at me. This man's mother said, "Did she just run into the wall?" I got right out of the car, walked around to the front of the car and said, "Yes I did just run into the wall, but everything is good." We have had several blonde moments together in our lives. Blonde moments, I believe, are spiritual *aha* moments in life, and it gives us a chance to laugh. I have so many blonde moments that I am the poster child for blonde jokes.

Since the beginning of our relationship, we set ground rules. We were not to lie to each other. We were not to cheat on each other. The important thing that we had to remember was to keep the line of communication open between us. If we had a conflict, we needed to deal with it and then move on. This was a lesson that I learned from my previous relationships. Our relationship was good most of the time; however, we had some conflicts. A couple of issues occurred early in our relationship that made me think we weren't going to last. They were small conflicts of betrayal toward each other.

I had put this man on a pedestal, telling myself he was not like all other men in the world. I felt as though he wouldn't be that man who would lie or cheat on me if I treated him right in the relationship. I believed that he would treat me with respect, love me unconditionally, and never do anything that would put a wound on my heart. This man was raised in a good home, and at the time, his mother was going through a divorce because her spouse had been cheating in the marriage. So, I thought for sure that he would never do this to me, because he saw the pain that was placed on his own mother's heart from this experience. The security, however, that I felt when I was with him was solid. This was the safest I had felt in any relationship.

One night, after our date, I ended up staying the night at his house. We were in bed the next morning when suddenly his ex-girlfriend came into his house, into the bedroom, and punched me in my leg. Oh, did anger fly through me, but I was able to keep my composure and not hit her in her face. I asked, "If you are not in a relationship with her then why in the hell does she still have your house key?" He was not able to provide me with an answer, which really made me wonder if he had truly ended the relationship.

That was it, I was not going to play games. I knew, or at least I thought I knew, that it was just not going to work. If the relationship was already starting on these grounds, I didn't want it.

After he told his ex to leave his house, I started packing my stuff. I felt as though he had proved my theory on men correct: all men are dogs. Those were my thoughts at that time because I had been hurt by so many men in my life. As I walked to my vehicle, he asked me to stay. He said, "Please don't leave. We can work this out." I didn't answer and kept walking. Then he said, "How many chances did you give your ex? Why are you not willing to extend the same to me?"

I sat in my vehicle, thinking about what he said. He

had made a very good point. This was the first time that he had hurt me and the first time that he was not completely honest about his relationship with his ex. I told him that he was only going to get three chances, regardless of how many chances I had given to my ex. I was not going to be in a relationship where there was no trust.

We sat for many hours discussing what was going to happen to this woman who just came into his house and assaulted me. I decided to go to court and file an assault charge. If I had hit her back, I would have gotten an assault charge for my behavior. I felt that it was important that even though she was mad at him, she should not use violence. That was strike one in my book of our relationship.

A couple more months went by, and everything was going great. One night, we were scheduled to go on a date after he finished work. I went to meet him at his house and pulled up to see his ex-girlfriend at his house on his front deck. He wore a look of, "Oh shit, I have been caught again." I was crushed. I didn't think that this man would do this to me, only because a couple of months ago he told me that it would never happen again. I had no idea if he had been still seeing her while he was seeing me or if she just wouldn't take the hint from him that he didn't want to be in a relationship with her anymore. I had hoped that she was the one who was pursuing him, still lingering around like there was hope for their relationship.

We had been having such a great time during the last month. I didn't understand why this woman was at his house. As I asked him why she was there, this woman started to explain that he had been coming to her apartment telling her that he was still in love with her and that she had a video of him on his knees asking for her back, that he wanted to give their relationship another try.

My heart shattered, broken once again by a man. I couldn't believe that this was happening. I asked myself, "Did I not learn my lesson? What did I do to this man for him to do this to me?" He looked at me with a serious face and asked me to leave. There was no goodbye, no I will talk to you later, no I am sorry, nothing. I was pissed at myself for allowing my heart to fall for this image of a virtuous man.

As I sat in my car crying, trying to understand why this had happened, I was in such shock that he would do this to me, but I knew deep in my heart that he was going to make it right again. The next day, he texted me asking if he could call. I was more hurt than angry because I'd never expected him to treat me like that. During our conversation, he explained that he had asked me to leave so he could finally end that relationship with his ex-girlfriend. He said the only reason he had gone to see her was because the relationship was familiar to him, which led him to fear our new relationship. I never could understand his logic. I thought our relationship was going great. He had complained about his last relationship and told me of all the things he didn't like about his ex. We were not rushing our relationship — we were simply enjoying being with each other. He apologized for putting me in that situation and asked if we could start over.

Strike two in our relationship book.

It was important for me to not introduce my children to this man until we had been in a relationship for six months. Since we had already started the relationship over twice, this rule was very important to me. We both agreed to this, especially because his ex-girlfriend had a child he had grown attached to, and we were overcoming some obstacles. We continued to date, and as the days turned into months, our relationship blossomed like a flower in the spring. Six months went by fast, and we reached the next level of the relationship. We agreed to continue seeing each other, which resulted in the introduction of my children.

During this time, I was still working nights at 7-11 and continuing my education to better my life. I was also dealing with a divorce, custody, and a new relationship. The emotional and mental toll that I was fighting inside was killing me. I was really trying to focus on the good things but was so overwhelmed with the stress that my depression returned. The only time I didn't feel depressed was when I was with my boys and my man. Every chance I got to spend time with him, I left my kids with my parents and went to his house.

This got very old with my parents. They were retired and wanted to enjoy their time together. They didn't want me to pawn my children off on them. I was taking advantage of them helping me, but it was not intentional. This behavior went on for about a year. Until, once again, my parents and I got into a fight. I needed to get my own apartment and really start being a mom to my children. I needed to put my children first and give my parents a break from me living with them. My parents had felt as though I was not raising my children or spending enough time with them. That I was not being the mother that I needed to be for my children. I was determined to show them that I was able to raise my children and be a good mother to them.

I was getting ready to rent a house for me and my boys. I asked him to come look at the house that I was going to rent. It was a three bedroom with a fenced-in backyard. The house was kind of old, but the price was just right. When we looked at the house, it was nasty inside. It smelled like cat urine, and the carpets were filthy, but I figured if I cleaned it up, then it would be a nice place to live. The house wasn't far from my parents, work, or my man.

As we stood in this house considering how much work I needed to put in for it to be a good place to raise my boys, he looked at me and said, "Why don't you and the boys just move in with me?" We talked about it for a while, bouncing ideas off each other, then decided after almost a year of dating, we were ready to move in together. We were moving our relationship to the next level. Our life as a couple with two kids was the start of a new journey together. Everything felt so natural. We were living like a family. Even people would look at us and say what a nice-looking family.

About a year and a half after I had met the man of my dreams, I realized that he was also battling depression. That was the first time I knew in my heart I was where I needed to be. I had suffered with depression in my own life. I had lived it, I had the damn t-shirt, and I wore it on Sunday nights. I needed to be there to help him with this, because he couldn't understand why he had these feelings. I thought that maybe it was because all his friends were married and had children while he was still doing the dating game. I do feel that spirit brings people together for one reason or another, some for a short time, and some for a lifetime.

I felt that I was supposed to help; however, I didn't really know how to help him. He told me he was lonely. His self-esteem had been damaged by his previous relationships. He was depressed because he expected to be married and have a family. I could be wrong, but this was the feeling I had at the time. I explained to him that I had been fighting depression my whole life. I pointed out things that he had going for him in his life, which helped him have a new perspective on his situation. I told him that he would have everything he desired in life if he maintained hope and faith that it would happen.

In our relationship, we were both able to provide different perspectives on situations that occurred that brought us closer together. We learned not to let temper enter in our conflicts. It was so awesome to be able to solve issues that came up. Although we have experienced some rough years, we are grateful that we still have each other. It was important for us not to have a relationship where we argued all the time. We had already experienced that kind of relationship and recognized that we did not want that for us.

Our house at the time was a double-wide mobile home. My man would work two p.m. to 10 p.m. One night, I decided to surprise him with homemade chicken wings for dinner. My youngest was in the kitchen while I made his dinner of chicken nuggets. I started to cook the chicken wings on the stove. I heated the oil to fry the wings when the oil caught fire and the kitchen went up in flames. I turned, looked at my son, and said, "Run outside, son, and stay on the deck."

I was in complete panic mode. I had just caught this man's house on fire. As I ran around the kitchen, trying to find where he put the damn fire extinguisher, I was so scared that I was not going to be able to put the fire out. I knew that he had an extinguisher; however, I couldn't remember where the hell it was in the house. I finally found the damn thing and put the fire out. I went back outside with my son's food and put him in the car so that I could call my man and tell him what had just happened to his house.

I just knew that he was going to be so mad that I had caught his house on fire. As the fire department was doing their job to make sure the fire was out, my man pulled up to the house. The first thing he did was to talk to my youngest son to see if he was okay. My son said, "Mom burnt the house up." Such a sweet boy.

I explained to my man that I was trying to make him some chicken wings for dinner, and the next thing I knew, the kitchen went up in flames. The only thing he said to me was, "Why did you put the fire out? I had insurance on this place." I was shocked. I totally thought that he would be mad at me for burning the kitchen down. We ended up getting everything straight with the insurance, and he got a new kitchen.

Several months went by, and I had an accident with my foot. I was not able to work since I was in a cast for my ankle. We had been out at a New Year's party the night before. I was going down a few steps into a room to give him a drink when I missed the step and tore several ligaments in my ankle. The drink went flying out of my hand, almost hitting him in the head. He said to himself, "She is throwing this drink at me. What in the world did I do to her?" Until he realized that I had seriously hurt my ankle and was unable to walk.

At that time, I was still going to school to get my degree. As soon as I was able to walk, I returned to working at 7-11; however, I changed my schedule so I was home at night. Our relationship was going so well. We worked together as a unit to raise the children. He was just so happy not to be alone. His entire demeanor changed once we moved to his house.

We were living the American dream.

As the years passed, I was able to complete my associate's degree. I was so pleased with myself for being able to finish my degree and had pride in myself again. I felt as though the sky was the limit. I had gotten my hope and faith back that I was finally on the right path in life. My life had become stable for the first time. My children were doing well in school. I was doing well physically and emotionally. I owed it all to my man for being my rock, the one who saved me from my darkness. We decided to celebrate my great achievements by going on a trip to Las Vegas.

This was very exciting for us, especially for me, because I had never left the east coast. We had never been on a long-distance trip across the country. I had never been to Vegas. My parents agreed to watch my children for a week so that I could celebrate the fact that I graduated from college and my birthday. As we were getting ready to go on the trip, I said to my man, "I can't wait to go to the beach in Vegas." Once again, he looked at me and said, "There aren't any beaches in Vegas. There might be pools, but no beaches. It's the desert!" He just laughed and laughed. Clearly, I hadn't done very well in geography; I barely passed it with a D-.

Once we got to Vegas, I was amazed by how big everything was there. A shuttle bus picked us up from the airport. The shuttle driver started to load our bags in the back of the bus. When he went to pick up my bag, not realizing that it weighed 100 pounds, my man didn't miss a beat. He looked at the shuttle driver and said, "Yeah, she had to bring the damn curlers with us." The shuttle driver laughed.

We ended up staying at the Luxor, which was the

pyramid casino. The hotel we stayed in was so beautiful. Prior to this, my trips had been limited to the east coast. I had been to Atlantic City for a company that I worked for in 2006, but this was completely different from anything I had seen before.

When we checked into the hotel, we received the keys to our room and headed up. As we were going up to our room in the elevator, I set our bag down on the floor of the elevator. I was so excited that I ended up leaving it in the elevator. The carry-on bag had our spare clothes, the camera, and our phone chargers. I was so mad at myself that when we realized that I had lost the bag, I was ready to go home. He looked at me and said, "We aren't going anywhere. We are going to enjoy our time together. Those are things that can be replaced, and we won't let this situation mess our trip up." Of course, he was right.

We ended up going to play some slot machines in our hotel first. I couldn't win a damn thing on the slot machines. I would put a dollar in on a penny slot and would lose it all. However, he would go to a Star Wars slot machine and win 50 dollars or more. I decided that slot machines just weren't my game. So, I decided to try my hand at blackjack. The coolest thing was that we didn't have to pay for our drinks while we gambled. We got so drunk sitting there gambling, not losing a lot of money, just having fun with each other.

We went to the Tropicana to try our hand at the blackjack tables there. I won hand after hand at the casino. We ended up ringing in my birthday at the blackjack table. I high fived every person who walked by me and I said, "Yeah! Guess what? Today is my birthday! High five." My man said I high fived everyone I saw. At one point, he looked at me and said, "Are we ever going to get back to our room? No, because you insist on giving everyone a high five."

Of course, as soon as we got back to our room, we both decided that we were hungry. So, I was going to go to the McDonalds in the hotel to get some food. As I left to get some food, he watched me walk through the hotel still high fiving everyone who passed me. He told me later that he said to himself, "She will be back in three hours with my food because she won't stop high fiving people."

I got in line at McDonalds only to find they were not accepting cards at the register. I was drunk as shit just trying to get some food, and I couldn't understand why the hell they were not accepting cards. So, I went to the hotel restaurant to get some food to-go. The hostess informed me that I could not order food to-go, that I would have to get a table and then order the food to-go. I was so mad that it had been two-and-a-half hours and I was still hungry. Another hour went by, and I was making my way back to the room with our food. As I opened the door, I noticed that my man had fallen asleep. I looked at him and said, "You better get your ass up and eat this food, because I just spent three hours trying to get it." We had such a memorable time on our first long-distance trip. This story is one that we tell at gatherings with friends.

Our relationship continued to grow so fast. In the blink of an eye, we had been dating for three years. My man is such a traditional man. We had started to talk about the possibility of marriage. He told me that he wanted to ask my parents for my hand in marriage. The day that he asked my parents, we had taken the kids to a medieval festival that was happening locally in the main square of the town. He approached my dad and asked him if he could marry me.

My dad said, "Yes, you have my blessing." He then laughed and added, "You can't give her back to us, either."

The proposal was prefect. We went to dinner at a very nice fondue restaurant. The meal was delicious, especially because they served cheese. (I am a cheese lover. I would probably die if I didn't have cheese.) As we sat at the table talking about our future, the waiter brought dessert. The waiter had written in chocolate sauce, "Will you marry me?" There were no words but "Yes." I loved this man as much as I loved my children. I felt as though he was my soul mate and God had brought us together for something great. This man had become my best friend, my lover, and now was going to be my husband. This was a magical night for me in every aspect possible. I never thought we would end up getting married. I never thought that I was able to be loved like he loved me. The whole day was perfect. The fact that he did everything that a man should do to prepare for marriage, from asking my parents to proposing to me, was the way I dreamed it was supposed to be.

The wedding planning began. We were not able to spend a lot of money on our wedding, but I wanted it to be beautiful. I was not one of those ladies who had to have a wedding that cost over 100,000 dollars. My wedding was to be small and more meaningful than anything. Every aspect of the wedding fell into place. Previously, I had bought a dress for $99, hoping one day I could wear it for my perfect wedding day. The venue was a chapel with an officer's club for the reception.

After the wedding, my oldest son was so upset to the point he was crying. It was hard for him to explain his feelings about the marriage. The problem wasn't that he was not happy for us, he was more concerned that it was too good to be true. Almost as though he was waiting for something bad to happen. At first, I just figured that it was happy tears for us getting married. It was happy tears, but he was also concerned that we weren't going to stay married. I was not aware of the damage and pain I had caused him when the marriage #2 didn't work out.

I felt so sad that I had put him in that kind of mindset to think that this relationship wasn't going to work. My son has loved my husband since the day they met each other. Their bond is unbreakable. They were video game buddies, they played Legos, and my husband had been there for my son when his own father wouldn't show up to support him in his activities. My new husband pulled him to the side and told my son, "I love your mother, and I will never leave you or your mother. I will treat her like she should be treated, and I will always be here for you. I love you, buddy, and you are my son." This conversation seemed to settle the conflict in our son's heart, which allowed him to enjoy the rest of the night.

It was a small wedding of about 65 people who showed up to be a part of our celebration of love. My husband and I assured our son that we were not going to get a divorce, that we were truly in love. We explained to him the different situations that I had endured during the last two relationships and that nothing like that was going to happen again. My son's face lit up for the rest of the night with joy that he was a part of this new life that we were creating together. The wedding was everything I dreamed it would be. It was beautiful and classy.

Our lives changed for the better. Instead of going on a honeymoon, we ended up using the money we received as wedding gifts to buy a bigger house and start our forever journey in life. Life was good. We were happy, and the family was doing very well. Don't get me wrong; we have had our ups and downs, but we never forgot how much we loved each other on our wedding day.

Shortly after we got married, we had our first big fight. I had found out that my new husband had been talking to his ex-girlfriend via text messages. He did this, I think, because he had found out that while we were dating and living together, I was talking to one of his co-workers over the phone saying inappropriate things that someone in a relationship should not have been saying. I don't know why I had done it, but I was very sorry and ended it before it truly started. At the time I did this, I was hurt by what he had done to me earlier in the relationship, and I wanted revenge. I know that was the wrong way to think in a situation like that, and since then, even when people have done me wrong, I will not seek revenge. It is not in my heart to be like that. We need to show love when someone hurts us. It was not my best moment, and I am very sorry that I did that to the man I love.

I was so hurt, done, angry that he would even talk to her — after all, we had just gotten married. I was angry at myself for believing that I could get married again. This was strike three in the relationship. I couldn't trust him. He couldn't trust me, either. We exchanged words, and I told him that it would be good for him to go stay with his mother and we would try to talk about this tomorrow. We decided that we were not going to give up on the relationship that we had worked so hard for just yet. We still loved each other very much. We figured that if we were able to gain trust for each other that we should be able to overcome any obstacle that happened in our life.

As I sat there reflecting on everything that had happened in this short period of anger, betrayal, and lack of trust, I started to get depressed again. I began self-medicating again to stop the pain in my heart. I fell back into doing pills, not Xanax or heroine. I was going to the doctor, giving the description of anxiety and needing something to take care of it so that I could sleep at night. The doctor prescribed me Klonopin, which is a sedative that numbs the body and induces asleep. Even though I was doing pills, I was still trying to maintain the life that we had started to build. However, I kept taking the pills, and my husband had no idea what I was doing.

I wasn't buying the pills — they were being prescribed to me by my primary care doctor. Until the day my husband had to take me to the hospital, because I had taken too many pills. I didn't overdose or anything; however, something just didn't feel right with me. When we got to the hospital, he found out what I had been taking and for how long. Knowing my past, he looked at me and said, "You need to make a decision. It is either the pills or me. One of us must go. Which one is it going to be?"

"You are right," I said. "The pills will go." Ever since then, I have not abused pills. I recognize now that we gave each other a fresh start in the relationship.

I began to understand that there was no need for me to be on pills again. My husband and I had made an agreement that we were going to help each other with our depression. It took this man who I loved to tell me that he was not going to watch me waste my life away in order to realize that I was worthy of living a good life with purpose. He was so right in that moment. It was as though a light bulb went off in my head. I was so blessed to have someone who could wake me up to see everything that I had in my life and what was to come for our family.

I had made sure that I told my husband that my tubes were tied before we got married. Just in case that affected his decision to be with me for the rest of his life. I made sure that he understood that there were options for us to get pregnant, but it was not a guarantee that I could produce a child for him. It was just in case he didn't want to marry me because I was not able to have children.

I would have completely understood if he didn't want to marry me because of this, since it was something he wanted in his life.

All he said was, "Well, it can be reversed, right?"

"Of course," I said.

Since my husband didn't have any children of his own, we decided to try to have a child together.

We scheduled the surgery for me to get my tubes reversed. This was very exciting for both of us. The thought of being able to have a child with this man was all I desired in that moment. The doctors were hopeful we would be able to conceive a child. We explained to the doctor that we wanted to try it naturally, and if it didn't work that we would consider IVF. As soon as we were able to start trying to have a baby we did. Everyone was excited in the family. Family members shared prayers and hopes that we were going to get pregnant immediately.

The first pregnancy was a chemical miscarriage. A chemical pregnancy is a miscarriage that occurs early in the pregnancy. This was the first time in my life that I had experienced a miscarriage. We had gotten our hopes up so high that we were going to get pregnant, only to receive painful news. I didn't understand how this could happen when I hadn't had any issues with my other two children. Our dreams were crushed. We didn't give up hope, though, that we would eventually get pregnant.

I felt as though I had failed at my wifely duties of providing him with his own child. This was a test of my faith, or so I thought. Doctors did more tests to determine the cause of the chemical miscarriage. They were not able to find anything wrong with my body or anything in my bloodwork that would indicate a problem. At the time, I had been under a lot of stress, financial stress, work stress, and dealing with the custody issues related to my second marriage.

I also put myself through high expectations on getting pregnant. I took a pregnancy test every time I was one day late. This went on for months. I would pray every time I thought that we might be pregnant and held onto hope that God was going to answer my prayers. Unfortunately, I was losing faith in ever getting pregnant again. We prayed every night to God that he would provide us with a child that we made from love.

Until July 2015. We got pregnant. The doctors were on point with medicine to help my body not reject the pregnancy. I have O- blood type, which means that my antibodies are high in my bloodstream and if something foreign is in my body, these antibodies attack. This includes attacking the fetus in my womb. If I have a miscarriage, I have to have the RhoGAM shot to prevent more miscarriages.

This was so exciting for us. We immediately started getting things ready for this baby, pulling out all the baby stuff that I kept from my previous pregnancies. It was still very early in the pregnancy, yet I had hope that we were not going to lose this baby.

While I was still early in the pregnancy, I was dealing with so much stress because I was still fighting a custody battle for my youngest son. We were in court when I started having bad pains in my abdomen. I had no idea what was causing the pain or if it was cramps. As I sat in the courtroom waiting to deal with the custody battle for my son, I was thinking in the back of my head that something was going wrong with the baby. A feeling of anguish came over my body, and the pain was not something that I was familiar with at the time. I made it through the court process only to return home to my husband with the pain I was having in my abdomen.

When I got home, I was in so much pain that I couldn't even stand up. We called the doctor who said to come to the hospital immediately. My husband wheeled me into the hospital and once the doctors examined me, they confirmed that we were experiencing an ectopic pregnancy. What is an ectopic pregnancy? An ectopic pregnancy is when the fertilized egg implants in the fallopian tube, which causes it to rupture the fallopian tube, resulting in internal bleeding.

I thought that breaking my leg was the worst pain, but I was completely wrong. This was not just physical pain, this was one more wound to my heart and soul. We longed to have a child together. I had prayed to God, begging him to give us a child. Broken, I began reflecting on whether I had said or done something to cause God to punish me with this pain of losing of our child. I struggled with these thoughts for several months that followed.

I'd had a feeling this child was going to be our little girl. This feeling was so strong, even though this happened early in our pregnancy. We had connected with her in the womb. We picked a name for our daughter. This was so very sad for us in our lives. All we wanted to do was give each other something that we had created together. I wanted him to be able to experience the magical moment of welcoming a child into this world. The joy of being a father and raising his child. My husband was so sad, I think sadder for me than for himself. He didn't know how to grieve the loss of a child who he had not laid his hands on. He was not able to connect to her like I had in the beginning. I wanted to talk about the loss, and he felt that it was too painful to talk to me about our daughter.

As a woman, I felt like I was a failure. I carried so much guilt on my heart because I felt as though I had caused this failed pregnancy. On a spiritual level, I felt as though I had done so many bad things in my life that God was punishing me. Probably because I had made the decision to have my tubes tied, which resulted in me taking away God's plans. The thing I struggled with the most was telling people that we lost the pregnancy. It was difficult simply because we were so excited to have a child.

There were some supportive people who came to offer their condolences for the loss of our child. However, some people blew it off as if it was too early in the pregnancy, a kind of "nothing lost, nothing gained" mindset. The family was compassionate with our loss; however, there are things that I feel should not be said after the loss of a child.

A few examples of what to never say to someone who just lost a baby:

> *"It just wasn't meant to be."*
> *"They are in a better place now."*
> *"God had another plan for your child."*

There is nothing that you can say to a mother and father that is going to make them feel better about the death of a child.

The loss of a child, even in the mother's womb, or if the child is an adult, is the worst pain anyone could ever endure. This unfortunate loss caused me so much pain, mental and physical. There were times my husband would lay in bed trying to hold me because I was crying so hard. He tried to help heal the pain in my heart from the guilt and blame that I held onto after losing our daughter. For the longest time, I couldn't even stand to be touched by him, not because he did something wrong, but because of my own insecurities. I blamed myself for not providing him with a child and felt that I didn't desire his touch.

I had to do a follow up with the doctor to make sure that everything was okay with my body. The tube had to be removed since it ruptured, and it was the one that was the better of the two. As I sat in the doctor's office, I had the gut feeling that bad news was coming again. The doctor looked at me and said, "We have to take the other tube, too. We are afraid if we don't, you will have another ectopic pregnancy."

I said to myself, "Man, Lord, I just can't catch a break, can I? How am I supposed to give this man a child if I don't have the equipment?" There was silence in the room as I sat there crying.

My heart was so broken yet again. Just another wound on my heart. My whole relationship with this man flashed before me as I saw it all coming to an end. I thought this would be the end of this marriage because I was not able to provide him with a child of his own. My age was 30 years at the time, so maybe there was still hope that we could have a child, but right in the moment it was a very unlikely event. The doctor explained not to give up hope, that there were still many options to get pregnant. It just wasn't going to be naturally.

The doctor stated that our best option would be to do IVF in order to have a child. My husband and I made the decision to wait a couple of years, because we needed to heal from the pain of our loss. I also needed to heal the physical aspect of my body as well. My husband was wonderful the whole time during all this trauma. He was so patient with me during my grieving process and continued to stand by me through all the healing of my heart.

My husband and I sat and talked for several hours about the options the doctor had provided for the future. We were tired of the emotional rollercoaster that we had been on for so many years. I told him that my body needed time to heal from all the trauma. He completely understood why I wanted to wait to try to do IVF later down the line. It was almost as if we knew that God wanted us to wait to try again.

Life continued after the loss of our child. The normal family things were going on every day. He was back at work. I returned to work. We were putting our focus on the two children we had in our lives with us. I was still kind of numb from the experience while I continued searching for answers from God as to why this had happened. My depression worsened. I had to put on a fake front to my friends and family, as if I were okay despite feeling like I had died inside. It was exhausting to go through the day and maintain a normal routine and not bust out crying. I buried the pain to handle the normal, daily family tasks.

Then our world was turned upside down again from an unexpected blow.

My husband's brother died at the age of 23 from a heroin overdose. My brother-in-law had been hanging out with the wrong crowd who took him down a path of darkness that he was not able to return from. The family had tried to help him with his addiction. He was sent to rehabilitation for several months on two different occasions. Our brother had so much anger and pain about his parents' divorce that he got involved with drugs to escape the pain. I knew exactly how he felt, I had been there in my dark moments. When we found out that he was using, we all joined in the effort of trying to help him to get off the drugs.

Since I was someone who had changed my life around with the help of family, I thought that he might listen to my experience to see that there was hope for a new life for him. One day I sat him down and said, "Even though darkness surrounds you now, the light that shines in you is brighter than the darkness that surrounds you." I tried talking to him about my experience with drugs and explained that the drugs were not worth throwing your life away. "Life does get better once you stop using the drugs." There are times I feel like I failed to help him, as if I hadn't done enough to help him.

This tragedy broke my husband's soul. My husband was 13 years older than his brother. It was almost like he had lost another child. We had so much guilt and blame because we couldn't help our brother during his illness. He was very close to his brother. Whenever his brother called, my husband was there for him. My husband loves his brother so much. It was a very traumatic time for the family. Our brother lived his life like it would be his last. He had touched so many people's hearts with his fun-loving, carefree heart.

Once, after his death, my husband was sitting on the bed in our room, grieving. He turned his head because he thought he felt his brother's spirit next to him. I do believe that our loved ones come and sit with us when we think of them or when we cry because we miss them so much. If we are able to have an open mind to our loved one's spirit, we can experience something supernatural in our own spirit.

My husband was mad at God for a long time for taking such a young soul from this world. The pain of losing his brother was so unbearable that he had lost all the life out of his soul. The pain that I had been feeling about the loss of our child was the same pain he was feeling for his brother. He talked about his brother often since he thought about him all the time.

After my brother-in-law passed away, our youngest child began experiencing supernatural things. Our son often said, "Mommy, I keep hearing knocking on my closet door." He also told me that he saw a shadow walking around in his room.

I asked my son, "How do you feel when you experience these things? Who do you think it is that is in your room?"

"I believe it is your brother-in-law, and he wants my help for something," my son said. At the time, my son wanted to share his experiences with my husband but was afraid it would be too painful to talk about.

It was hard for me to hear my husband talk about his brother so much while he was unable to talk to me about the child we had recently lost. I felt we needed to talk about that loss, too. I needed to hear from my husband how he felt about our daughter, and I knew that the pain I was experiencing needed to be shared between the two of us. But at the time, I set my feelings aside so that I could help him heal his broken heart. I understood that my husband had a beautiful relationship with his brother for many years and I just needed to be supportive during his grieving process.

During this time of heartbreak, I was able to be present for my mother-in-law in a way of healing because I knew the pain that she was feeling. It was not the same pain, but nevertheless, I understood. There were nights where we would sit there trying to figure out how her son's life got so bad that he felt that this was the only option. She had plenty of friends and family who surrounded her with love and prayers. Yet, that was not what she wanted. She wanted her son back, she wanted to hug him, kiss him, help him in any way she could. She felt as though she had failed as a mother to him. One thing I have learned on this spiritual journey is that our tears are meant to heal the wounds of our hearts. We spent many nights holding each other and crying over our loss.

In the midst of this tragedy, I reconnected to my spiritual side and recognized that God does have a plan for us. I was not sure what my purpose was going to be in this life based on everything I had gone through. The obstacles we endure in our lives place us in the right place at the right time. We are all spiritual beings in search of our destiny. The journey is our spiritual awakening. We experience things that happen in our lives to provide us with clues to our spiritual awakening. These clues allow us the opportunity to return to our sacred path of spirituality.

Shortly after my husband's brother passed away, his

grandmother died. His grandmother's health had been decreasing for months. She was 85 years old and had lived a very blessed life. This woman was what I called a straight shooter. When we decided that we were going to get married, she gave me a brochure that she received from church about the commandments of marriage, the do's and the don'ts. She was a loving woman who accepted everyone with open arms. Her passing became another wound on our hearts. Three deaths in less than two years. I remember my husband would ask me how much more pain would we have to go through in this lifetime, as if I were able to predict a future tragedy to better ready ourselves.

It was not an answer I could provide to him. The only thing I could do was hold him like the many nights he had held me during my pain.

I have always felt as though I was on a different universal plane spiritually from everyone around me, only because I have experienced supernatural moments that have no explanation beyond the supernatural. Almost as though I was psychic in some way. Things have happened in my life that I first saw in my dreams and then they become real. I always thought it was spirit providing me a warning of what is to come.

As we continued our life after picking up the broken pieces of our shattered hearts, we went through the motions, completely numb to any emotion that surrounded us. I knew deep in my heart that things were going to get better. I had faith that it was going to get better. At that point, we were so broken that there was nowhere else but up for us. We buried our sadness so that we could seem normal around friends and family, even though we had not completed the cycle of grief. We were still able to continue with life while hoping for our dreams of better times to come true.

Chapter Six
A Best Friend's Betrayal

Since I came to live in Virginia, I have had friends who have come and gone in my life.

Husband #3 introduced me to one of his childhood friends. My husband's childhood friend was married to a woman who enjoyed the same things in life that I did. We went on vacations together and weekend parties. It was good to have a couple we could hang out with on the weekends. We never thought the friendship would end. It was told to me as a child that if you can count the friends on your hands who will stick with you through everything in life, then consider yourself blessed.

While we were friends with them, we would go to concerts, NASCAR races, and travel together. We would often hang out on weekends, having backyard fires and beer. As our friendship continued, we started to notice some changes that made us feel as though they were using us for their own benefit. We felt that they were not showing us the same courtesy that we had extended to them during our friendship. My husband and I put it out of our minds, thinking that we were just assuming things that weren't really happening.

My friend and I always talked about working together in a business. We would sit for hours plotting what our business was going to be. One day, she informed me that the business that she worked for was eventually going to be sold.

Ever since I was a child, I have always wanted to own a business. My friend, who had been a part of our family for many years now, told me that the business where she had been working for 15 years was looking to sell. The business had been operating since the 1980s. The business owners were older and wanted to retire. She informed me that the way the business owners had been operating the business was out of date but that we would be able to turn it around to make a lot of money. The business had not had a price increase since 2008, which caused them to lose money on the inventory where the cost of material had increased. They also had not done any advertising for the business since it had been opened in the 1980s. There wasn't a lot of traffic going in and out of the store.

My friend told me the details of the business. I felt as though this was God giving us an opportunity to have the life I finally wanted and to be successful with this business. I was grateful for the opportunity to run my own business. There was so much money I thought could have been made if we were to make small changes, based on what I was told by my friend.

This is just a piece of advice: If a business opportunity should ever come up dirt cheap, check their financials. Also, get trained in the services of the business before buying the business. The other advice I have is don't ever go into business with one of your friends. All it takes is one disagreement, and the next thing you know, you have lost a friend. I feel as though I should have done more research on the kind of business I was purchasing prior to buying the business. This was a hard and costly lesson that I learned.

However, I was so excited about having my own business and helping my friend keep her job that I was bound and determined to make it work. I felt as though I was doing the right thing for both of us. Everything fell into place: the funding to buy the business with the help of family, the lease, and the staff to run the business. There were things that needed to be changed and upgraded in the business that were easy to fix. I should have seen the signs from the beginning.

Shortly after I took over the business, my friend and I got into a fight which didn't end well. The impression that I got was that she had a problem with me being the boss. As a first-time business owner, I was in the shop learning how the business operated daily. My friend just wanted me to buy the business and let it run like it had been for so many years. She didn't want me to make any changes. All she expected me to do was pay the bills and do the marketing for the business. However, she didn't seem to realize that the business had been failing for so many years because the business owners were simply letting the staff run the business. The staff offered discounts while the price of the material increased. It was later brought to my attention that the previous owners were behind on their Federal and State taxes by $10,000 or more. The only way I found out was that I was in the shop when the call came in looking for the previous owners. I couldn't believe that I had just been screwed over this business. I know that she knew this was happening to them, yet she encouraged me to buy this business to save her ass from having to find a new job.

While in the shop, I noticed that the other employee locked the door in the middle of the day when the shop was supposed to be open. I had customers telling me that this lady who helped them with their purchase smelled like alcohol. It got to the point that when I asked about it, she decided to quit. That made my friend mad because she said that I forced her to quit.

As anyone can clearly see, this was not the case. I was a new business owner, and the staff was responsible for using blades, framing equipment, and dealing with customers. Drinking on the job was a liability issue. My friend was supposed to have my back like I had her back when I bought this business. We had been friends for seven years, and in the blink of an eye, I watched it going in the toilet. When she betrayed me by badmouthing the store, this had a major effect on business. Everything started to go downhill.

We were losing so much business that we weren't making enough money to cover the overhead. So, I made the difficult decision to shut the business down. I was already in so much debt that there was no way we were going to able to recover. I have heard from other business owners who had failed businesses that this happens more than people know and to not get discouraged. Their advice was if the business is failing, then shut it down, don't continue to lose money. The greatest businesspeople in the world have had at least one failed business or more under their belt. Now I was part of that group.

I was so hurt and couldn't understand why my friend would have betrayed me after all I had done for her and her family. It was just another wound on my heart. I felt that there was a lesson that I was supposed to learn during this process. In my opinion, the lesson was that even though a person is your best friend, only trust them so far. We might think they have our best interests at heart, when truly they are only thinking about themselves. I am the type of person who thinks of other people before myself. It was just so naïve to assume that others think like I do.

Again, I went through a death in my heart. Not the physical death of my friend, but a relationship death. For me, it was unheard of that the loss of a friendship had the same grief process as the loss of a loved one. I have grieved for the death of this friendship as if I lost my sister. It is important to forgive the betrayal of anyone who has done you wrong in your life. God teaches this in the bible. If you are not able to forgive, how do you expect to be forgiven?

Forgive, and let the pain leave your heart.

Chapter Seven
Our Last Chance

Though my heart was hurting, my husband and I decided that we were going to try IVF.

We started the process of doctor appointments, ordering medication, and preparing for the procedure. I was excited and scared at the same time. Several questions rolled around in my head. What happens if we have multiples? What if it doesn't work? What is my husband going to think if I can't get pregnant? Are we ready for another disappointment?

I kept these questions to myself while remaining optimistic for my husband, all the while praying that it was going to work out. As the process of IVF started, there was already complication after complication. First, a side effect of the medicine is that it causes a cyst in the ovary. The cyst needed to be drained so the eggs could grow. Then, my hormone levels were not where they should have been while on the medicine. The eggs did not grow to the proper size, and treatment was stopped.

This information was so disheartening. We had already pulled the money from my husband's retirement fund to pay for the IVF. Our biggest concern was if the egg didn't develop, then we would not be able to truly start the IVF process. There were so many things to consider that we were overwhelmed.

The medicine cost so much, and we only had one shot to make this work. We ended up saving some of the medicine for the next cycle. We waited until the following month to start treatment again. We prayed and prayed that entire month as we wanted to start IVF again. During the waiting process, I reflected on my life decisions. If I hadn't gotten my tubes tied, would we have our children by now? Had I truly interpreted God's plan for me and my family? We went into the IVF process with all the hope our hearts could hold about having a child together.

I felt it was an obligation to get pregnant, because my husband was now the only heir to his mother. We wanted to give her a grandchild so badly. She has two grandsons, my boys, yet it is not the same as having one of your blood lines. Plus, my husband had no heir to carry on his last name. I wasn't sure exactly how my husband truly felt about the thoughts that rolled around in my head, and I really didn't want to think negatively about the situation.

We ended up getting further along in the second IVF treatment until the medicine caused another cyst in my ovary. The cyst resulted in us losing the eggs before we could even extract them for fertilization. At that point, I was crushed. We had used up all the medicine on that cycle and could not afford to try again. The disappointment I felt was just so horrible.

After that happened, we sat on the front porch one night, talking about the events of the day. My husband turned and said, "This is it. We are done with trying to have children. I am good with the life that we have built, and thank you for everything that you have been through to try to give me a child."

I must be honest: all the worry, stress, and pain of us trying to have a child was released when he gave me his blessing to stop trying. I felt as though the pressure of this world lifted off my shoulders. Our souls had been damaged so much that we knew we needed to focus on us. This gave us the opportunity to heal together.

That was the hardest conversation I believe I had to have with my soul mate. The guilt that I carry about not being able to provide this amazing man a child because of a decision I made when I was 22 was overwhelming.

All I wanted to do for him after the loss of his brother was provide him with a child in hopes of filling that hole in his heart. I have not completely lost hope that one day I will be able to provide him with a child.

Daily, I reflect on our child that we lost. Just wondering what she would look like physically or what her personality would be as she grew up with her brothers. Plus, all the joy she would have brought to both sides of the family after so much loss and pain. There are times when I can feel her presence and the presence of all our relatives who we have lost in the past years.

When there is a loss of someone we love, our soul longs to feel them again. Just have hope and faith that they are there with you, and then you will start recognizing that they are with you always.

Chapter Eight
My Spiritual Journey

*E*verything that has happened in my life is designed for spiritual growth.

There were times when I struggled to have faith and hope that everything was going to work out for my family. At times I lost my path to God. When we have hope and faith, we experience miracles that help us reconnect to our spiritual journey. As we walk on this spiritual journey as women, we need to remember to give back to ourselves, to love ourselves. We need to love our bad decisions along with our good decisions in life. Thank yourselves for the life you live. I have been able to find my spiritual journey and recognize that the lessons I learned have made me the person I am today. That for every emotional rollercoaster I rode in my life, I learned something deep about myself and the spiritual growth that I accomplished.

All my life, I have been so lost in what happened to me as a child that I failed to realize the good that has surrounded me. I always had a deep feeling that I am meant to share my life with people as part of my soul's purpose. To provide a roadmap for the people who are lost in this world. Because at times I have been lost as well. I failed to look at the path that provided a bigger picture. I have maintained through my life for the most part my belief in God or some form of a higher power. We are all God's children in this world, we all have the spirit in our soul that needs to be ignited so we can help our brothers and sisters.

I have sinned in my life — please don't think that I feel Godlier than anyone. I am a humble person who is grateful for the blessings that my creator has placed in my hands. However, I have looked to the sky and said to God, "This is a misdeal, and I would like a different hand of cards dealt to me, please."

I had no idea how powerful spirit can be when trying to reach the hearts of the people in this world. We all cross each other's path for a reason. They come to teach you things about yourself that they may have learned on their spiritual journey that could give you new insight on your spiritual path. Embrace these moments with honor and share your experience with the next generation.

I have been blessed with a friend where our paths have connected. My friend has opened my eyes once again to my soul and what my purpose is in life. I have always had a feeling that I am supposed to help children with some of the things that I experienced in my life. To help them learn the lesson from their pain but to see the blessing that has been revealed. She is a Traditional Native Guide to Spirit. This beautiful woman is the most incredible soul I have ever met. She can connect with spirits who have passed or, as she calls it, crossed over. I would like to share my experience with a spirit communication she performed for me and my biological mother.

I had been feeling like it was necessary for me to communicate with my biological mother to answer the questions that haunted me my whole life. This communication was meant to help me to heal from the pain of my childhood and to receive a roadmap or clue to help me find my purpose in life. My questions included:

"What am I supposed to do in my life?"
"What is my purpose?"
"Why did she give me up for adoption?"

That last was the biggest question I wanted answered. During the spirit communication, my friend, my mentor on this spiritual growth journey, spoke of things that no one would possibly know but me or my biological mother. There was a message I needed to hear from her to ease the pain in my heart. To start the process of healing the deep wounds that she had created while I was a child.

This was the start of my path to my soul. The path that was going to advance my spiritual growth to a new level. I found out things I needed to do for myself. I received confirmation that I had felt the presence of my mother around me when I called on her. I felt that there were items that my biological mother had left behind after she died as clues for me to learn more about who she was as a person. My friend told me that the reason she gave me up was because she had mental issues, but she was able to keep it under control in public. I was told that when my biological mother was pregnant with me, she knew there was something special about me, but she was not going to be able to provide me with the life that I desired. My friend also told me that she had left something for me after she died, and that I should get in contact with the person who had the items. I was also told to spend time with my biological mother's friend who had her items because she had stories to tell me about my mother.

I decided that it was important for me to include the one mother who has always been there through all the pain and good times of my life to join me on this quest. I had hoped that this journey would allow my adoptive mom and me to connect on a different level of our relationship. I wanted to share in this experience in the hope that my mom might understand the struggles and the internal battle that I had been fighting for so long. At the time, I hoped that maybe I could help heal the wounds that I had placed on her heart.

We started our trip where it all began, in Florida and Georgia, with hopes of finding answers I had been longing for my whole life. My biological mother had a very good friend who lived across the street from her shortly after she gave me up for adoption. We visited her to see if she could answer my questions about why I had been given up for adoption or if there were any items left behind when my biological mother moved out of the house. I learned that after giving me up for adoption, she dealt with issues of marital infidelity, emotional abuse, and suicide attempts. All things that I had gone through during my childhood and adult life. It amazed me that we were connected this way, that we shared these aspects of our lives. Of course, I feel as though this is the generational chain that I hope I have broken for my children. The friend had also saved a teddy bear that my biological mother had purchased and her address book that had her handwriting.

My adoptive mom and I learned that my biological mother had misunderstandings about me. Because of these misunderstandings, she had relayed false statements to my adoptive mother. My biological mother's friend also told me that my mother loved me very much and wanted the best for me in my life, which is why she gave me up for adoption. I received many blessings on that trip. The biggest blessing was to share this spiritual journey with the one mom who has carried me emotionally, physically, and spiritually from the age of eight until the present, even though we sometimes have conflicts between us.

The healing and information that I learned about my mothers, especially with my mom who adopted me, gave me more insight than I could ever have hoped for. I love my mom dearly for the relationship that we have created in the last several years. It has been a slow process but the foundation is getting stronger every day. My entire life, all I ever wanted was to be loved unconditionally by my mom. However, the misconception was on me.

I realize now that my mom has always loved me unconditionally; however, I was so focused on the pain of what my biological mother did to me that I was not seeing the loving mom I had in front of me. During my life, I have believed that there was a higher being or higher spiritual plane that I needed to tap into to reach my goals in life. The ability to dream of the life I wanted and then to manifest it into reality was a skill that I needed to capture. Almost like magic. There have been times in my life where I would pray for something I wanted or needed, which then would become reality.

So as part of my spiritual journey, I started to investigate this so-called magic to manifest the desires of your dreams. The things that I discovered about manifestation were amazing. My research led me to start practicing the manifestation of my dreams. I started receiving messages in my dreams, not of my desires, but of more clues for this spiritual journey. Every night, I learned new things about myself and how it related to my spiritual journey. I have since started a dream diary so I can interpret and understand the meaning behind my dreams. There is a message in our dreams that our spirit is trying to speak to our soul so we can be the person we want to be.

I have found that a higher power, whether you call it Creator, God, Buddha, or whatever you call the higher being in your life, is in control of our spiritual journey. That the root of the higher being is spirit. I feel as though spirit is the voice that tells us when something is not right with a situation, spirit is the butterflies in your stomach you get when making a life decision. My experience of these feelings has provided me with signs as confirmation of spirit within myself.

History has taught us that there have been many different religions throughout the world. People have always had a sense of some form of religious belief in their life. I have noticed that when going to different religious rituals, there is always one common factor for me that resonates with my soul. I feel it is the spirit in my soul that guides me through life. I pray to God, Creator, and my ancestors to guide me through the next chapters in my life, and I have faith that they are going to place me where I need to be to fulfill their plan.

At this point, the population of the 21st century are all connected through our ancestors. Everyone has ancestors who connect us in one way or the other within the world. Our ancestors were more connected spiritually than we are today. Everyone longs for something magical to happen in our lives, or even a miracle, if that is what you call it. Our ancestors are here to help heal our hearts by reflecting on the lessons and blessings in our lives that we have learned.

Begin to heal your wounded hearts. Be grateful for who you have become and what you have in life. If we teach children to have gratitude for the small things in life, then they could dream bigger and achieve even more. I have always said it takes a parent to teach our children. It takes a community to raise them. We need to teach our children the ways we were taught in past generations from our ancestors. The pain and suffering of lessons are our ancestors teaching us their wounds of the heart so we can carry the lessons to the next generations to grow spiritually. We are all different melting pots blended into one: "The Creator."

As I reflect on my life, I am now able to recognize the many lessons of my ancestors, people around me, and my personal lessons of life while teaching my children the ways of spiritual growth on their own life journey to break the chains of past generations. It has been very important for me to share my spiritual journey not just with my children, but the children of the world. I have learned that having patience allows time for me to absorb the lesson and find blessings in every experience. The tongue is more hurtful than physical pain. Yet if we hold onto faith and the hope of something bigger, we become limitless.

We need to teach our children to be kind and to have unconditional love for every human being. Since I was a child, there were times when I had hatred in my heart that only made me bitter toward other people. I have since realized that this is not a pain I want to carry in my heart. God loved me when I was abandoned. God loved me when other people in my life judged me for my past. God loved me when I placed judgement on myself. God loved me through my bad decisions and my achievements. My spiritual journey brought me to recognize that I have never been abandoned.

Judgement is not for mankind to place on our brothers

and sisters. Judgement is for God and only God. We must come back to the original teachings that God wanted for his children. When people are divided, that leaves room for evil to place a seed; when our hearts cry, it will water the seed of evil. Let God tend to the garden of your heart so that you can reap the harvest that he has planted in your life. Everyone must go through darkness to find the light of our soul.

Take a moment and think about your life. When times were rough, who did you call on? The first thing that most people do is pray, whether it be to God, Creator, the Moon, Mother Mary, or whoever you have a connection with, while maintaining hope and faith that there will be relief for the situation happening in your life. We always seek the high power at some point in our daily activities. People want to believe in miracles. All God wants is for us to ask for that miracle so we can guide our brothers and sister who are spiritually sleeping back to his heart.

I have always felt as though there was a hand guiding me through the experiences I have chosen to go through. It was not God's plan for me to suffer the pain that happened in my life. However, there were lessons I needed to learn in order to fully see the blessings that God had planned for my family. During the times of my darkness, where I felt as though I would never recover, there was always a sense of optimism that helped me come out of that darkness. God wants to share his love with us, and I feel that during our times of darkness, we feel his love the most.

Many people have crossed my path and educated me about different religious beliefs that have been in their family for decades. I have found my own way to have a relationship with God. I have attended various churches and received messages that moved my spirit. I feel as though too much emphasis is placed on religious denominations as opposed to spiritual beliefs.

For example, someone could read a poem, and God will use that poem to awaken your spirit and place peace in your heart. Or there might be a song that comes on the radio that will make you cry in order to heal from the pain in your life. If we were to be more aware of the signs that God places in front of us, we would only have beauty surrounding our life.

During this journey, I have been able to find harmony in my life. My heart is at rest with the pain of the abandonment, the sexual abuse, the emotional abuse, the physical abuse, and the betrayal. It has become my goal to help people who have been through the same situations in life. To help them see that even though God has allowed this to happen, we are to use this experience to help others.

The children of this world are our future. We need to

stop killing our future children and give them the tools they need to grow spiritually. If we teach our children that what they dream will come true through the power of God, we could change the world for the better. All God wants is our love. Our love for him, our love for his creation, and our love for our brothers and sisters.

The definition of spiritual growth is to have a higher awareness or to develop higher consciousness. When we sit in silence, or go for a walk in the woods, if we pray, or if we meditate, we are accessing the higher awareness of the consciousness. This allows us to come closer to God with our dreams and desires. Your dreams and desires are made possible by God.

I have sat for many days, meditating on life. As I look around outside, I am in complete awe that God created every living thing on this earth by simply speaking it into existence. From the ashes of the darkness, he can provide rebirth of our soul. It is like the dead leaves that fall in autumn to fertilize the flowers for spring. The women with wounds on their heart are the dead leaves to fertilize the flowers for our children.

It is important to reflect on our life to continue the spiritual journey so we can receive healing and blessings to pass it forward for the next generation. If we allow evil to rest with our spirit, it surrounds us with conflict, drama, pain, and suffering, but if we live in the light, our spirit will shine so brightly it will cut the darkness into pieces. It took me a very long time to learn this message. For so many years, I have lived with evil in my heart for all the wrongs I endured during my life. It consumed me to the very core of my soul until I was awakened by the light of spirit once again.

We allow evil to consume our heart at times. During times when life is not what you want it to be, evil is present. If you are miserable with your job, or unhappy in a relationship, you are struggling financially, evil is working to break your spirit. I learned to find the blessing in situations in my life that have allowed me to grow spiritually to help someone that God put on my path for the day. For the longest time, I fought the evil inside of me by physical methods instead of fighting it spiritually. During this journey, I have been able to identify evil's presence and change it in my life.

We dwell in evil sometimes, and that affects the choices we make during the day. This can manifest in how we speak to people when we are angry, even though they haven't done anything to us; fighting with your spouse because of something small that could end up making them end the marriage; arguing with children, placing bitterness in their heart toward their parents. These are all signs of evil.

I have been blessed that God has allowed me to have

five different lives. It seems as if every time something was not going right in my life, I would pray for a fresh start, a do-over that God granted me, including the blessing of having two beautiful children and one who is with God in heaven. I can feel her more and more every day while I write this book.

I have taught my children to be grateful for what they have in their lives, even if it is the smallest thing given to them. This allows them to give to others. You never know if there is going to be a time when someone will pay it forward back to you.

We should not be defined by race or creed. We are described as our Creator's children, humanity, and we all bleed red. Our religious belief, our hair color, our skin color, and our culture are what make us Creator's children. We need to inspire people to be more than what they see themselves as. If we stop putting labels on people and start looking at their hearts, we would be united once again in God's image for this world.

I have taught my children many things, but one that has proven to be important in my heart is to dream big, and with prayer, all things are possible. They have learned to take words of discouragement and use it to motivate them to achieve their dreams. Even now, as I write this book, there are people in my life with discouraging words toward my goals. This has allowed me to stay focused on what I want for my heart. If the light of the spirit is left to fight the evil feelings, then we can live in harmony with God and Spirit and travel the path that is planned for us.

The heart is the gateway to our soul. If we don't listen to the heart, then we will not hear the cry of our soul. We will remain in misery. For generations, we have been taught by our teachers, elders, and parents that it is crucial to have an education, a good paying career, and financial stability to have a great life. Yet, we can have a rich life with what is placed in front of us by the hands of God and Spirit, so listen to the desires of our heart.

Today's society is focused on the materialistic lifestyle of this world. The big house, the nice car, the new trend that is out. If all these things were to disappear in the blink of an eye, would we still have the things we need to survive in this world? Our ancestors lived a simple life, a humble life, a life of prayer and worship to a higher reality. They were grateful for the plants and the animals they were able to eat. They were grateful for the shelter that protected them during a storm. All they had was faith and hope that everything they needed was going to be provided to them by someone greater than they were. I have been able to reconnect to that higher reality through my spiritual journey that has placed me back on the path of my soul.

Recently, I have been encouraged to investigate my

ancestors and heritage. I was not surprised to find there is Cherokee in my bloodline. This is the root of my spirituality, the original teachings of my ancestors that I must reconnect to, so I am able to help in the future by teaching my children and my children's children the path to their own spiritual journey. Everything we see in nature is a message from our ancestors' spirit. If we can open our hearts and minds to the endless possibilities of this world, we will no longer be trapped in the misery of our soul.

I know there are times when it is hard to continue to live with the pain that has been present in our lives. But we need to use that pain to fight for the souls who are lost on their spiritual journey. If we dwell in the pain, it will eventually kill us. The pain doesn't go away; however, it becomes easier to deal with daily. Fight through the pain to see the blessing, and you will start to feel peace, love, and knowledge that you are going to survive.

The lowest points in my life were all because of me telling God that I was in control, to only be led back to him in prayer to be saved from the trauma in my life. This has been the pattern since I was born. My search on this spiritual journey is never ending. I end up learning something new either about myself or this world that we live in every day. This is a beautiful thing to be able to realize all the magic and miracles that surround us.

Now, I am constantly receiving confirmation from spirit that I am on the right path. That if I speak to spirit that of which I desire, it will be granted to me at the right time. In my past, I have had to learn patience when asking for the desires of my heart. As a child, I could not understand why I had to wait for these things to present themselves in my life. I was a child who wanted it now — right now. If I didn't receive it from someone, then I would go and get it myself. This impulsivity and lack of patience caused me to make bad decisions in my life.

While I have been on this spiritual journey, I have researched many different religions, including Wicca, Baptist, Catholic, and simply utilizing the spirit to find information. I have had palm readings and card readings, attended women's circles and other spiritual ceremonies. During my various enquiries into religions, I had been intrigued to learn more about the Native Americans, witchcraft of the light, and Celtic old religion. During all the spiritual ceremonies I have participated in, I left with the feeling of goosebumps and that I had already done these ceremonies. Not in my current life but almost as though in a past life. It has been told to me by my elders that these feelings I received is the spirit within the soul awakening.

The one ceremony that stood out for me was my sacred path reading. If you have experience or understand what a card reading is, then you will know that your energy is placed on the cards. You then draw your card, and the interpretation begins with the drawn card. As my hand hovered over the cards, I was pulled to one card out of 25. The sacred path reading deck consisted of native symbology. The card I pulled contained three different messages for me. The first is the number 27. Each number has a positive and negative spiritual meaning. The picture was of a native cradleboard with a baby. The third message pertained to what to do with the information, and the statement was "Ability to Respond."

I will start with the numbers and relay their meaning. The number two in its positive aspect is feminine, dreams, and cooperation. The negative aspect of the number two is sensitivity. So, the teaching shows that a feminine energy is trying to teach me through my dreams and needs my cooperation to be open to receive my messages. The negative is being sensitive to discouragement in my life or in my choice of career or what my title is in this world.

The number seven aspect of positivity is wisdom, seeker, and soul. I need to have the wisdom to seek the true purpose of my soul, it is for the seven generations of the past and the seven generations to come. Passing my dreams on to the next seven generations of my family. All women are healers of this world. Women are givers of life not just by women (you do need a man), but to give birth to the new generations. The negative aspect of the number seven is being too critical of myself. I should always focus on the positive in life instead of the negative, which I do all the time. However, there are times when I doubt myself and do not speak my truth. That is because of the discouraging words that I received during my life. If we can recognize the negative, then we are able to call it out and change it for the good. The other piece of the negative seven is to have more faith in our dreams. Stop focusing on the why of life, the what, and the how that consumes the thought process of your plan.

If you speak your life goal, spirit will bring the items necessary for it to bloom. We must have faith in the face of doubt from others. It has been stated to me from Chinese proverbs that, "When the journey becomes the destination, then you have reached enlightenment." This really helped me to open my heart up more to faith and to really focus on all the people that I have encountered in my life.

When I saw the picture of the native cradleboard, it reminded me of how I have chosen to protect my children while still allowing them to follow their heart's desire. The definition of a native cradleboard is a frame or a board on which an infant is secured. It is wrapped with fur and handmade blankets. It is considered a portable cradle that allows people to carry an infant from place to place. I have visualized and placed my hopes and dreams in a cradleboard to keep them safe until it is time for them to be shared for the process of healing mankind.

The last part of the sacred path card reading is the "Ability to Respond." I have noticed in my life that I am quick to go straight to a defensive mode with my comments. This is a trait I work on every day. I strive to speak words of kindness; however, there are so many people with disconcerting words that I want to counterattack them with my own. It is a defense mechanism that everyone has in their heart, especially people who have been hurt the most. Spirit helped me learn to respond with love and not hate, to understand that people have hate which stems from fear. If we can remember to speak with love and not hate, we will be able to live united once again.

This spirit journey has been so amazing for healing the wounds of my heart. I am so grateful for the healing that I have received from everyone who walked with me on this beautiful journey. There was a time when I felt as though I was not going to make it through all the pain and tragedy of this life. While I have been on this path, I have found myself, not just for me but for my husband, my boys, and my family. I do not look at myself as a victim of my circumstances, but as a survivor of the internal battle waged within my heart.

Despite my life's struggles, I have still been able to fight for my truth. Although I was abused, the emotional and physical pain seems to not hurt anymore. The further I go on this spiritual journey, the faster I heal every day. The support that my teachers, my children, my husband, and my family provided have taught me to breathe through moments of adversity while still having the courage to jump into the opportunities that present themselves in my life.

It is such a great feeling to be able to let go of the pain and begin to relish the joys of my life. I feel as though I have been reborn into the largest library of spiritual growth. Every day, I learn something new about my ancestors, be it through prayer, meditation, or dreams. The knowledge is contained within our soul; we must want to seek the teachings. We all long for something better in life, we just don't know how to get to the center of our soul.

It is very important to be open to anyone who steps onto your spiritual path with you so you can learn something new about yourself and the world around you, enabling you to become one with yourself. Because of the tragedies in my childhood, adolescence, and adulthood, I recognize the several constant themes I experienced. Those themes include the strength I was given to sustain me; even in tragedy, I have been able to pull through the storm with my belief in God. I have always had a guardian angel near me. I can overcome any conflict or situation necessary. Finally, the love of spirit has surrounded me always.

My hope is that when people read this book, they can reflect on their lives and find the lessons that will allow them to change their outlook and fight for their truth. Hopefully, they can view the blessings that God or Creator placed in their lives. All of creation was made to be good with the understanding that evil does surround us, but we can choose not to indulge in the evil forces. We must have the strength to stand up to evil and say it is not welcome here.

Just as a toddler in daycare will play with a child who is different from them, they know no evil, just love for the other person. If the world set aside all the racism, hatred, and fear, we would not have so many wounds on the hearts of our mothers. Remember what your mothers taught you as a child: treat others as you would want to be treated.

We are all children of God, and spirit is our mother. I believe that this is the feminine divine energy that lives within us. This is what causes us to become emotional about something when we go to church or worship. During these times, we open our hearts and minds to seek more information about the higher spiritual realm.

There are light walkers upon this world who work

to help elevate the knowledge of our spiritual journey. When you hear that a person is the life of the party, that is because they have harmony with the charisma of spirit while being carefree, like a child's love for life. We can reconnect to our spiritual reality if we take the time to be open to the possibility of something bigger and better for our soul. It is then that we learn our life's purpose.

We are all here to do something great for this world; something great not just for ourselves but for our neighbors as God intended. If we listen to our hearts and soul while doing the work of our ancestors, we will be filled with a sense of peace.

I hope that this book can help people who need to know that they are not alone in their life experiences. My wish is that everyone can find their path and continue their spiritual growth journey.

I leave you with one last thought:

If we were created in God's image, then our spiritual journey begins in the womb of our mother's wounded heart. Let's start healing our hearts as well as the hearts of mothers around the world.

I am a Butterfly Warrior.

I am a Master in Spiritual Growth.

About the Author

Tina Edens has been a resident of Virginia for 29 years and lives in the Tidewater area. As an avid believer in the power of faith, love, and prayer, Tina decided to create a written testimony of her spiritual journey to help others find healing.

Tina's many jobs and career paths helped her prepare for her life's purpose: to share her story of the struggles, happiness, and pain that led to a healing of her heart. Tina loves to read spiritual healing and growth books, and her goal is to inspire others to continue to heal and start their spiritual journey.

Her intent for "A Mother's Wounded Heart" is her words light the way for others throughout the world who have faced trauma in their lives and work, enabling them to overcome those obstacles.

More information can be found about Tina at:
Instagram: amotherswoundedheart
Twitter: @amotherswounds2
Facebook: www.Facebook.com/motherssupport4u

www.ingramcontent.com/pod-product-compliance
Lightning Source LLC
Chambersburg PA
CBHW030151100526
44592CB00009B/219